Test-Taking
Power
Strategies

NEW YORK

Library of Congress Control Number: 2007933550

Printed in the United States of America
9 8 7 6 5 4 3 2 1

ISBN: 978-1-57685-633-8

For information on LearningExpress, other LearningExpress products,
or bulk sales, please write to us at:
    55 Broadway
    8th Floor
    New York, NY 10006

Or visit us at:
    www.learnatest.com

Contents

▶ How Can I Get Smarter than the Tests I Take?

Check the following questions that you want answered by this book. You will find the answers in the chapters indicated. A summary of the answers can be found on page 177.

MULTIPLE CHOICE (CHAPTER 7)
_____ Why are so many tests made in this format?
_____ How do I choose between two answers when they both seem correct?
_____ Which should I read first, the question or the answers?
_____ How do I handle choices like "all of the above" or "none of the above"?

TRUE/FALSE (CHAPTER 8)
_____ The statements always seem true to me. How do I know when a "true" answer is really false?
_____ Sometimes part of the question seems true and another part seems false. How do I know which to choose?

MATCHING COLUMNS (CHAPTER 8)
_____ Why do instructors sometimes put more answers than questions on a matching column?
_____ When two answers are very similar, how do I know which one to choose?

IDS, FILL-INS, OR COMPLETIONS (CHAPTER 10)
_____ How much information is required? I never know how much to say.
_____ What do I do if I know the answer but have forgotten the spelling?
_____ What do I do if I remember only part of an answer?

ESSAY QUESTIONS (CHAPTERS 11, 12, AND 13)
_____ Why are essay questions so popular?
_____ How do I make sure I don't run out of time when I write an essay answer?
_____ How do I figure out what to prepare before an essay test?

IN GENERAL
_____ When—and how—should I guess on a test?
_____ How much time should I spend preparing for an exam?
_____ If I have to cram for a test, how do I do it?
_____ Should I study with other people?

Introduction

HOW TO USE THIS BOOK

So, you have to take a test. Is that a test—or a TEST!? No matter how many tests you have taken, you probably feel a little grip of anxiety at the prospect of taking a test. You're not alone.

Most teens get a bit stressed when they have an exam coming up. This book is here to help. It has been written expressly to help you overcome any test-taking anxiety you may feel and to help you become a savvy and effective test taker.

▶ WHAT TESTS ARE YOU GOING TO TAKE?

There are many kinds of tests that you may have to take. Here are the most common:

- Standardized tests include the General Educational Development® (GED®) Tests, SAT Reasoning Test™ (SAT™), and ACT®. A passing grade on the GED gives you a high school equivalency diploma. The SAT and ACT are college entrance exams.
- Classroom tests measure how well you've learned particular information and techniques and skills in courses, workshops, and the like.

Let's look at two general categories of tests.

STANDARDIZED TESTS

Some tests are standardized tests, where a person's performance is judged against the performance of hundreds or thousands of other people who have taken the same test. In other words, a standard of performance has been established and each test score is measured against that standard.

Some standardized tests measure *achievement,* or knowledge acquired in a particular area of study. Some familiar examples would be:

- Comprehensive Tests of Basic Skills (CTBS), which are exams children take in school
- General Educational Development (GED), which are exams taken to acquire high school equivalency certificate

Other tests measure *aptitude,* or the ability to learn certain tasks. The most obvious example of such a test is the SAT.

Standardized tests are used for placement, class rank, promotional decisions, or entrance to training programs. Most of these tests follow a multiple-choice format. Answers are generally recorded on a bubble grid in pencil and are scored by computer (see Appendix A, "The Answer Grid").

This format is favored by creators of standardized tests because it allows an objective standard of performance. This means that the creators of tests can't change the test to offer an advantage or a disadvantage to a particular group of test takers.

NON-STANDARDIZED TESTS

Non-standardized tests seek to measure how well the learner performs on tasks that are related to the particular curriculum of a course. Classroom tests are a good example of non-standardized tests.

Classroom tests are often made up of a number of question-and-answer formats that may include multiple choice, true/false questions, matching columns, fill-ins, and essays. This kind of test is more flexible and allows greater leeway for instructors to emphasize particular topics and to assign grading weight where they think it is most appropriate. Some instructors even wait to assign point value to some areas of a test until the test has been given. This enables them to decide on what that value should be depending upon how well the largest numbers of students did on each section. The test also functions as an evaluation of the instructor's effectiveness. The instructor is, in fact, using the test to guide an assessment of how well he or she taught each section tested by the exam.

On the following page, think about your own experiences as a test taker and learn a little about the learner you are.

▶ WHAT KIND OF TEST TAKER ARE YOU?

Check the following sentences that best describe your test-taking ability.

_____ **1.** I am always nervous about tests.

_____ **2.** I am nervous about tests only when I don't feel confident about my performance.

_____ **3.** Sometimes, the more I study, the worse I do on exams.

_____ **4.** If I have the time to study, I score better.

_____ **5.** I do best on tests when I cram for them.

_____ **6.** When I take a test, I want to know the results immediately.

_____ **7.** When I take a test, I don't want to know the results immediately.

_____ **8.** When I get nervous on tests, I freeze up.

_____ **9.** I do better on essay questions than on short-answer questions.

_____ **10.** I do better on short-answer questions than on essay questions.

_____ **11.** I do better on tests when I study alone.

_____ **12.** I do better on tests when I study with a friend.

_____ **13.** I study better when I am in a quiet room.

_____ **14.** I study better when I can hear the radio or television.

_____ **15.** Sometimes, I am surprised when I get a lower score than I expected.

_____ **16.** Sometimes, I am graded unfairly.

_____ **17.** I sometimes get a better score on a test than I expected.

_____ **18.** I sometimes do better on standardized tests than on classroom tests.

_____ **19.** I sometimes do better on classroom tests than on standardized tests.

_____ **20.** I sometimes study the wrong things for a test.

My worst experience with a test was when

_____

because

_____

My best experience with a test was when

_____

because

_____

1

Finding Out about the Tests You Must Take

Y ou can't prepare for a test until you know what test you'll be taking and when it will be given. If you are planning to go to college, you will probably need to take the ACT or SAT as part of your application process.

▶ HIGH SCHOOL EQUIVALENCY TEST

If you don't have a high school diploma, you can take the General Educational Development (GED) exam to earn a similar certificate. This exam tests for knowledge in each of the key curriculum areas typically found in high schools. It's a very important test for anyone who expects to move on to higher education.

The GED is developed and administered by the Department of Education in each state. The official website is www.gedtest.org. Schedules of exam dates are available online, at public libraries, or can be requested by writing to your state's Department of Education in your state capital. GED tests are administered at designated schools and agencies across the country.

You'll find preparation guides to the GED at libraries and in bookstores. GED preparation classes are offered at community colleges and high schools. Check online periodically and watch the newspaper for notices of continuing education courses and GED classes near you.

▶ COLLEGE ENTRANCE TESTS

Most colleges require all applicants to submit their scores on one of these assessment tests—either the SAT or the ACT. They may specify which one or give you your choice; it often depends upon where you live and what college you're applying to. Some colleges may also require one or more of the standardized subject tests known as the SAT Subject Tests.

SAT

The SAT measures your general ability to do college coursework, by measuring your verbal and mathematical reasoning abilities. The SAT Subject Tests (formerly known as the Achievement tests) measure your mastery of secondary school subjects.

The SAT also includes a Student Descriptive Questionnaire that allows students to give information regarding their interests, educational objectives, and academic background.

Registration materials for the SAT and SAT Subject Tests can be obtained from a local high school, at the website, or by writing:

The College Board SAT Program
P.O. Box 025505
Miami, FL 33102
www.collegeboard.com

ACT

The ACT is another standardized test that's used to prove readiness for college coursework. It's required in place of the SAT by a number of colleges, particularly in the Midwest. The ACT includes tests in math, English, reading, and science reasoning. The scores on all four subjects are averaged together to give an ACT test score, which is more or less equivalent to the SAT score. ACT also has a battery of tests under the ASSET program, by which colleges test students in reading, computation, algebra, and language skills for purposes of placement.

Registration forms for the ACT can be obtained by mail from:

ACT Registration
P. O. Box 414
Iowa City, IA 52243-0414
www.act.org

Fees for taking the SAT and ACT are waived for those who can provide proof that they are on public assistance.

TESTING TIMES

SAT and ACT exams are given several times a year. They are held on Saturdays, but those who cannot take Saturday exams for religious reasons may apply to be tested on the Sundays following the scheduled exams. The SAT takes three hours 45 minutes to complete, and the ACT takes three hours. SAT Subject Tests each take one hour.

TOEFL

The Test of English as a Foreign Language™ test is required by some schools for students whose previous schooling was in another country. Information about TOEFL® is available by mail at:

Educational Testing Service
Rosedale Road
Princeton, NJ 08541
(609) 921-9000
http://www.ets.org

You can also find information about TOEFL online at www.ets.org.

▶ CLASSROOM TESTS

With classroom tests, teachers and professors schedule tests and examinations at specific times during the year, either in the classroom or another specified room.

Classroom tests often contain a mixture of short-answer questions, multiple choice, true/false, fill-ins, matching columns, and essays. Most instructors want to:

1. Assess students' understanding of facts and information easily and quickly, which is best done with short-answer questions
2. Judge students' understanding and expression of larger concepts of class discussions and assignments, which is best shown in extended answers or essays
3. Provide students with a form of review, so that instructors can see where students' weaknesses are and what they should study more
4. Improve students' test-taking abilities

▶ PLANNING FOR A STANDARDIZED TEST

Be sure you know about the test well in advance. Once you know when an exam is to be given, send for the application immediately so that you will have plenty of time to complete it and return it in time for the test.

After you get a copy of the application, follow these steps to complete the application process:

1. Make at least one copy of the application before you fill it out. Then, you will have a spare if you make an error in filling it out or if you lose it.
2. Read through the application for a description of what will be tested.
3. When you are applying to take an exam, keep a file with all the papers pertaining to that exam in a safe place. It is very easy in busy households to lose or misplace important papers. Many exam packets contain a number of forms, such as admissions cards you'll need to get into the examining room and special instructions for completing the application. They are all important.
4. Be sure you know whether a personal check, money order, or certified check is required for test fees. Make a copy of the check and keep it with your other records.
5. When you are mailing applications and checks, it's a good idea to send them by registered mail or with a return receipt, so you get proof of when the application was received. Keep such return receipts with your records.

For most standardized tests, you can register online.

▶ PLANNING FOR A MAJOR CLASSROOM EXAM

You don't have to apply for classroom tests—they come automatically with the class! But you will want to find out exactly when they're scheduled so you'll be ready for them.

1. Check your course outline or syllabus carefully to note when the midterm and final exams will be held.
2. Immediately write down the dates of major exams in your home and pocket calendars.
3. Make sure you have copies of all class notes, handouts, and texts that you need for the test.
4. Make a copy of your important notes and leave this second set at home in case you lose the originals.
5. Plan your schedule around the exam dates, and allow plenty of time for study and review.

In a world where nearly every life experience is going online—from listening to music to shopping—can virtual testing be far behind? There is little doubt that within the next few years more and more testing will be done via computer. Today, many students already use computers to take tests by e-mail or on interactive websites. Classroom tests can be put on disks for students to take at home or in school computer labs.

GENERAL HINTS FOR TAKING ANY TEST ON A COMPUTER

1. Feel absolutely comfortable with the machine.

   If you work on only one program at work or school and perhaps use your home computer mostly for word processing, you should think about spending some time learning how to use other computer programs, websites, and other Internet resources. Most public libraries have computer access and staff who can help you navigate past the basics on an unfamiliar machine. It would help to practice until you feel truly confident that you can find your way around several programs.

2. Manage your time wisely.

   Time management is important for all test taking, but there are specific situations that are part of taking a standardized, *timed* test on the computer. Take all the time you need studying the tutorial you are given at the beginning of the test. Most tests have a Help function available throughout the test, but usually, the time spent being helped is time away from the test. In addition, some tests have a time crawl on top or below the text, alerting the student as to how much time he or she has left. If this is distracting to you and makes you more nervous, you should simply hide the crawl and rely on your watch to measure your time on each section.

3. Take charge of your own test.

   Make an educated guess. Making educated guesses is so important on a test that penalizes poorly chosen answers, so be sure your guesses result from a savvy elimination of choices that are likely to be wrong. We talk about this in detail in Chapter 9. On a computer test, where you don't have the ability to physically cross out your eliminated answers, you can do the same thing on the scratch paper you are given at the test site. Quickly jot down 1-2-3-4 or a-b-c-d on your paper, and cross out the options as you eliminate them. This will narrow your choices and allow you to concentrate on picking the answer most likely to be correct.

   Front-load your time. Because the computer will base its selection of questions on your responses to the first few questions in each section, be sure you spend the longest time on those questions. Don't linger over later questions, because you need to be sure to answer all the questions in the section. Make your educated guesses and then move on. But give a bit more time to the earlier, pace-setting questions that are more important to the level at which you will be working and, therefore, to your overall score.

Be comfortable in the setting. Just as in any other test-taking situation, give yourself the advantage of wearing comfortable, layered clothing. Have tissues, gum, and cough drops handy if they are allowed. If you are relying on your watch to keep the time, be sure you have a new battery in the watch or that it keeps accurate time. Follow the other suggestions included in this book about rest, exercise, and mental preparation for the exam.

Later chapters will go into more detail on planning for a test and managing your study time.

On the following page, fill in the information needed for the kind of test you expect to be taking. Check your answers on the sample answer page that follows.

IN SHORT

You need to be prepared to take any test. First, find out what test you need to take: the GED, SAT, ACT, TOEFL iBT, or classroom test. Then, obtain the information you need as soon as possible so you can begin to prepare for the test.

TEST PLANNER

Exams I must take this year

_____

Exams for this course are currently scheduled for

_____

Filing deadline

_____

The location of this test is

_____

I will find information about this exam by checking the

_____

People I know who have taken this course or test

_____

Three things I need to know about this test are

_____

_____

_____

TEST PLANNER

(Completed sample)

Exams I must take this year

ACT

Exams for this course are currently scheduled for

November 10

Filing deadline

October 1

The location of this test is

George Washington High

I will find information about this exam by checking the

Information in my guidance counselor's office and www.act.org

People I know who have taken this course or test

Joe Martin—friend

Three things I need to know about this test are

Do I have to bring ID?

How much math is on the test?

Is there a good test-preparation book available?

YOU NEED A PLAN, AND THIS CHAPTER WILL TELL YOU ALL YOU NEED TO KNOW TO PUT TOGETHER AND CARRY OUT A STUDY PLAN THAT WILL HELP YOU PREPARE FOR THE TEST OR TESTS YOU HAVE TO TAKE.

Making and Carrying Out a Study Plan

Preparing for a test is most effective if you have a system that keeps you focused on a very specific goal. And your goal, of course, is to get the best score possible. As in most things in life, the more you plan to succeed, the more often you will succeed. Don't rely on luck and savvy. With an important test, it's just too risky. Staying casual about your exam, playing the procrastination game, and only dabbling with a study plan could sabotage your chances of success.

Taking a test is a lot like taking a trip. The better it's planned, the more pleasant the journey. While you may say that you like to be spontaneous and let the spirit move you in taking off on a trip, you may find that you wind up with no place to stay, you've brought the wrong clothes, and you're trying to do too much in too short a time.

The same thing can happen with a test. You may find that you've given too much priority to studying minor topics, that you haven't managed your test-preparation schedule well, or that you lose your momentum partway through the test itself. This chapter guides you step by step through the process of setting up and carrying out a study plan for a standardized or classroom test.

▶ STEP 1: SET A TIME FRAME

STANDARDIZED TESTS

Most standardized tests are given only a few times a year, so you'll need to get those dates and plan around them. You should allow anywhere from *two to six months* to prepare for a test like the GED, ACT, or SAT.

CLASSROOM TESTS

For a major classroom test, such as a midterm or a final, you need to determine your preparation time according to several factors:

- **How much does the test "count"?** If a major test counts for half or a quarter of the final grade, you will want to allow about two weeks ahead of the test date to prepare. Some finals or midterms count the same as other exams. If that's the case, you will need to review a little each day for at least a week.
- **How many other tests are you taking at the same time?** If you are taking several tests in a short period of time, you need to make a schedule that will assign a reasonable amount of time to each of the tests, quizzes, and papers that are due. (More about this later!)
- **What is the test worth to you at this moment?** In other words, how well are you doing in the course right now? What does this test mean to this course? If you are achieving an "A" in the course, you may want to spend less time because you have already demonstrated progress in the class and have a good grasp of the subject. If your earlier test marks in a particular class are low, you'll want to plan on a longer preparation time. You'll need to spend extra time studying the material.

▶ STEP 2: GET THE CORRECT INFORMATION

STANDARDIZED TESTS

Check filing dates for the standardized test you need to take. Find out if you will be taking subject tests on the same day. Check your testing kit. Read the directions and suggestions for success that come with the papers you receive with the sample test.

CLASSROOM TESTS

Check your calendar to see whether you have other tests at or near the same time. Ask the instructor about the format of the test: Is it going to be short-answer or essay? Will you do it in class or take it home? Find out how long the test will be and what specifically will be covered. Assess how much the test means to your final grade.

▶ STEP 3: GET ALL YOUR MATERIALS

STANDARDIZED TESTS

Find some review books or other materials you may need to prepare for the test. You can find test-preparation help for most standardized tests using a search engine such as Yahoo! or Google. Find out if there are any test-preparation courses available to you in your community.

CLASSROOM TESTS

Look over your notes to be sure they are clear. If they are not, try comparing notes with another student. Finish any reading or other assignments you may have missed. Check to make sure that you have all handouts. Ask your teacher what will be covered on the test.

▶ STEP 4: STAY ON YOUR PLAN

Treat yourself to an afternoon walk, a candy bar, a long phone chat with a friend—anything that will reward you for maintaining a good study schedule. It isn't easy, and you should pat yourself on the back when you can stick to your routine for some period of time.

▶ SAMPLE STUDY PLANS

Because each type of test is different, each should have its own study plan. Here are some examples to get you started thinking about what you will need for your study plan.

STANDARDIZED TESTS

This schedule is for an important and comprehensive test that requires lots of preparation time, like the SAT or ACT.

Four to Six Months before the Test

1. Request all materials needed for the test.
2. Buy a large desk or wall calendar and enter the test dates for your test.
3. Browse the bookstores or libraries for review books or CDs that contain sample tests. Buy or borrow only one or two that seem appropriate. Too many books can be expensive and overwhelming. Note what other resources are

> **Whose Books Are They?**
> Don't be tempted to borrow textbooks or review books from another student to save money. When test time nears, guess who will be the one with the book? The one who paid for it—of course!

available to you through the Internet or from print material. (See Appendix B "Additional Resources" at the end of this book.)

4. Analyze the format of the test. Is it all multiple choice? How many questions are in each section? How long does the test take?

5. Take two sample tests from a review book. Check your scores on the tests. See how you performed on each part of the test. The strategies you are learning in this book should help you complete even these practice tests more successfully.

6. Write down the two areas in which you scored the lowest on both of the two practice tests: math, spelling, reading comprehension, and so on.

7. Do two more subtests for each of the areas in which you scored lowest.

8. Based on these early practice sessions, decide if you need help. For example, do you need to work with a tutor or perhaps take a review class in math or English?

Eight Weeks before the Test

1. Set aside one hour a day to review the test areas you want to improve. Do just the parts of each test you want to work on—as many as you can do in an hour—for four days a week. Do a complete review test three times a week.

2. Keep a chart or graph of your scores on the review tests (see p. 183). Take note of your progress. Are your scores going up? Are they uneven?

3. Organize a study group with others who will be taking the test. There are some drawbacks to this, but study groups are helpful to some test takers.

Four to Six Weeks before the Test

1. Confirm the date of the test.

2. Confirm that your application has been received and that you have been sent all the necessary materials.

3. Make sure you know where the test will be held and how you will get to the test site.

4. Continue to review for half an hour to an hour five days a week. Notice that, contrary to expectations, you are spending fewer hours a week in preparation. If you have been reviewing regularly for a couple of months, the reviews should take you less time since you're so accustomed to the questions. This is the most important part of preparing for tests. The more familiar you are with the test, the better you will perform under testing conditions.

5. Meet with your study group. Encourage each other; a positive attitude is a big help.

One Week before the Test

1. Take two more review tests. See how your scores compare with the tests you took at the beginning. Don't become anxious if you do less well than you think you should at this point. The reality is that you *do* know more than when you started, and it will show when you actually take the test.

2. Concentrate on being well rested and relaxed about the test.

3. Make sure you have all necessary items—pencils, watch, calculator, ID—and have arranged for plenty of time to get to the test site.

CLASSROOM FINAL EXAMS

Naturally, classroom tests differ according to the subject matter, the purpose of the test, the number of students being tested, and the preference of the instructor. Your preparation will depend upon how well you're doing in the class, your level of interest in or importance of the subject matter, and how much time you have to devote to this subject.

Large classes, especially in math or science, may take tests on separate answer sheets that are electronically scored. Other tests in the humanities and social sciences may require extended answers and essay questions that will be graded by the teachers.

The following is a sample study plan for a final exam in the ninth grade.

Two Weeks before the Test

1. Review your grade status in all your classes.

2. Review your grade status in this class.

3. Review the syllabus (course outline) to find out what percentage of your final grade depends on this test. Ask the instructor whether the test will cover the entire term's work or just the material dealt with since the last test or the midterm.

4. Ask about the format of the test. Will it be short answer, essay, or a combination?

5. If you missed any classes, photocopy a classmate's notes for those classes. Collect any handouts distributed by the instructor.

Ten Days before the Test

1. Review all textbook reading. Read margin notes and the text that is highlighted or underlined in the assigned chapters. Review all class notes. Borrow a set of notes from a classmate, and make a copy of them.

2. Arrange for at least one study session with another student. Compare notes with that person and discuss possible areas of emphasis on the test.

3. If you are uncertain about any aspect of the class and if there is a lot riding on this test, this would be a good time to make an appointment with the instructor to clarify any parts of the material you don't understand. Be sure that you take your class notes and a list of at least three specific questions to the meeting.

One Week before the Test

1. Create study notes from text and class notes. Make flash cards. Begin intensive study of factual material: dates, names, facts, and terminology. Use study strategies from Chapter 3.

2. Write out possible extended answers to essay questions.

3. Outline answers to help organize information in your mind.

Two Days before the Test

1. Review notes and handouts.

2. Reread text notes.

3. Reduce notes to a handful of cards or pages that can be used for quick last-minute review as you work on other courses.

One Day before the Test

1. Review notes and assigned reading material one more time.

2. Eat well and exercise. Go to bed early.

3. Face the day with confidence!

▶ THE TEST-PREPARATION BOOK MARKET

There is an enormous market in test-preparation or review books these days. The study plans we have outlined in this book assume that you will spend at least some preparation time working through or consulting commercial review materials. When you go to the store to purchase your review books, however, you may find that the huge selection is overwhelming. In addition, because the cost of a review book is generally somewhere between $15 and $25, you may want to be sure that the books you purchase are going to meet your needs. Here are some tips for selecting review materials.

- **First, think about yourself as a learner. Ask yourself these questions:**
  How much *experience* do you have taking important tests?
  How *important* is this test to you?
  How much *time* do you have to use a review book? *Where* will you be using the book?
  What *kind of text* appeals to you? (Do you like a chatty, informal style? Do you like a more serious, no-nonsense approach?)
  How much can you *spend* on review materials?

- **Now think about the book choices you have. Ask yourself these questions:**
  What does the book look like? What is its format, size, and general content?
  Most review books are paperbacks that are intended to be consumable. That is, the publishers expect the books to be written in and used up. Some are 8.5-by-11-inch books, small enough to fit into a bookbag or briefcase. Others may be 9-by-12 inches and three to four inches thick. The larger books may be difficult to keep with you outside of your main study area.

Some books are quite visually appealing. They have cartoons, lots of wide margins, and text and print that are shaded to highlight important information. Some are full of strategies and tips for dealing with test questions. They may have appealing icons that appear regularly in the text to alert the reader to important strategies or testing tips. Other books have denser text and expect the test taker to discover the methods he or she needs to deal with different testing tasks. Some books have relatively little to say about test-taking strategies, but provide a great deal of practice material.

Ask others who have taken the test for recommendations on the books they used to prepare for the test. Don't ask to borrow someone else's test-prep book. The whole idea is to practice putting in your own answers. You don't want to confuse yourself by looking at how someone else answered the questions.

What is the author's writing style?
If you are going to spend several weeks working your way through a review book, you should select the writing style that fits your approach to the test. For example, some review text writers employ a breezy, conversational, humorous style. These writers invite the reader to prepare for the test almost with a sense of personal competition with the test makers. This kind of approach is often appealing to young people or test takers who like to feel that they are outsmarting the test writers. These books may also be helpful to those who are especially anxious about testing and find that the informal tone makes them feel more relaxed and confident. Other test takers prefer a more business-like approach that allows the test taker to practice without much guidance from the author. While at the bookstore or library, skim through a few pages of a prospective test book to sample the writing style. Choose the "voice" that speaks to you.

Does the book offer extra features that may be helpful?
No doubt because of the keen competition in the test-preparation market, many publishers of review materials include add-ons with their books as an incentive to purchase the material. Such extras include computer software bundled with the book, discounts for computer-based practice materials, guides to college applications, and test-preparation timelines. Check out the extras. If they don't apply to you, then the book may not be a good choice to meet your needs.

A WARNING ABOUT REVIEW BOOKS

Classroom test takers, beware of using the test-prep book as a substitute for fuller study. Students taking courses in certain subject areas may benefit from using a review book in math, biology, or grammar to enhance their general knowledge of the subject. But be careful of using one of the "Notes" books, instead of, for example, reading *Moby Dick* or *Madame Bovary*. Most instructors are very much aware of the kinds of questions included in those books and may be very suspicious of essays that sound as though they were copied or adapted from those materials. In addition, each teacher will have his or her own take on the themes, characters, and plot lines of the novels they teach and will want to see those ideas reflected in the work submitted by their students. Use the "Notes" books to reinforce, not to replace assigned reading in class.

AT THE BOOKSTORE

The best selection of test-preparation materials is usually found in the large chain bookstores. The benefit of those stores is that they allow you to spend as much time as you like browsing through the books. Take your time and be selective about the materials you choose. Here is a systematic way of sampling the offerings.

1. **Pick out two or three books** that look interesting, and find a corner where you won't be in the way of other browsers.
2. **Skim the whole book first.** Note the format, print size, and numbers of practice tests included in the book.
3. **Read the introduction to the book.** Get a feel for the guiding philosophy of the writers or publishers.
4. **Check the publishing date** to make sure you have the most recent edition of the book.
5. **Read through the directions and through the first few pages** of at least two of the review tests. Make sure you can follow the directions easily and that there are enough practice tests to help you, but not so many that you feel discouraged about getting through the book.
6. **Think about your own specific needs for review.** If you need to review particular content—math skills, grammar or history, for example—you may want to buy a smaller, general review book and also purchase one or more of the skill guides that are available.
7. **Think about how you intend to use the book.** Will you be using it as your primary review source or as a reference book for extra practice around other review resources on the Internet or in a test-prep class? No need to buy the larger, more comprehensive books for spot review.

The hardest part about making a plan is actually starting the plan. On the next page, you have an opportunity to outline a plan for your test or tests by thinking through what you want to know about the test and how you can get prepared to do your best. Compare your answers with those on the completed sample study plan that follows.

YOUR STUDY PLAN

In the following space, write in a schedule for the two months prior to taking a standardized or classroom test.

The test I need to take is

_____

It will be held on

_____

The test site is located at/in

_____

Three questions I have about the test are

_____

_____

_____

I plan to study for this test as follows:
Two months before the test

_____

One month before the test

_____

Two weeks before the test

_____

One week before the test

_____

Two days before the test

_____

The day before the test

_____

(Completed sample)

In the following space, see a completed sample of a study plan for the two months prior to taking a standardized or classroom test.

The test I need to take is
Biology final

It will be held on
Dec. 15

The test site is located at/in
Room 104

Three questions I have about the test are
Will my lab grades count?
Will it be multiple choice?
How much does the test count?

I plan to study for this test as follows:
Two months before the test
Make sure I have the handouts and notes since midterm.

One month before the test
Keep up with reading assignments. Do all labs and look at finals schedule.

Two weeks before the test
Check my grades in this class against other classes.

One week before the test
Create study notes, study with group. Outline chapters, make maps.

Two days before the test
Memorize phyla, other basic facts. Create final study notes.

The day before the test
Review notes and go to bed by 11.

▶ CARRYING OUT YOUR STUDY PLAN

Here are some suggestions for carrying out your study plan to its successful conclusion.

LOCATION, LOCATION, LOCATION
Find a quiet spot, use a good reading light, and turn the TV and radio off.

Find Quiet Places
Your quiet spot may be in a different place at different times of the day. For example, it could be the kitchen table early in the morning before breakfast, your school library, or a corner of the sofa late at night. If that's the case, make sure your study material is portable. Keep a folder or bag that contains your notes, practice tests, pencils, and other supplies. Then you can carry your study materials with you throughout the day and study in whatever quiet spot presents itself.

If quiet study areas are nonexistent in your home, you may need to find a place elsewhere. The public library is the most obvious choice. Some test takers find it helpful to assign themselves *study hours* at the library in the same way that they schedule dentist appointments, class hours, household tasks, or other necessary uses of daily or weekly time. Studying away from home also minimizes the distractions of other people and other demands when you are preparing for a test.

Lights
Libraries also provide good reading lights. For some people this may seem like a trivial matter, but the eye strain that can come from working for long periods in poor light can be very tiring—a cause of fatigue you can't afford when you're studying hard. At home, the bedside lamp, the semidarkness of a room dominated by the television, or the bright sunlight of the back porch will be of little help to tired eyes.

Many of the review books that contain sample standardized tests have small print, often on newsprint-style paper. You need a good light just to see what you are working on!

About That TV and Radio
Certainly, if you have a TV or radio playing in the room where you are studying, it is not going to be a quiet place. But many people swear that they can't concentrate in a room that's too quiet. They need the background noise of a television or radio to screen out the smaller noises generated by the life going on around them.

If you do enjoy some sound in your study environment that's not just the beating of your own heart, however, be selective about the times you study with the TV or radio on. The TV or radio may be a good companion when you're reviewing old notes, writing study cards, or otherwise gathering information for study. However, silence is golden when you're trying to memorize, taking a practice test, or thinking through a math example.

Remember that there won't be any television or radio in the background when you're actually taking the test. It's probably a good idea to get used to working on test material in the same general atmosphere of quiet in which you'll take the test.

PARTNERS IN PREPARATION

Once you have a study plan in place, you may also want to consider the roles of other people who are involved with your preparation for the test. Your friends may not understand why you can't go to the movies with them the weekend before your exam.

Or, your family may not realize that you have to forego the weekly trip to Grandma's for Sunday dinner because you have to study.

Keep Them Involved and Aware

Here are some ways to get support from family members and friends during study time:

- Let your family and friends know what you need to do. Share your study plan with them.
- If your study plan covers several weeks or months, sit down with the people in your life, and work the plan around everyone's important needs. Look at the calendar together, and plan your study or reviews so that they don't interfere with significant events such as holidays, important family gatherings, or work obligations.
- Keep a calendar with the details of your study plan where everyone can see it. Then anyone who needs to can look on the calendar to see when you will be busy. They may be less likely to put extra pressure on you at those times.
- Ask for help. Even young children can help someone to study. Family and friends can quiz you on facts you must memorize, talk through difficult ideas, and take over some of your chores to give you time to study. Don't be afraid to ask for help, and then let people help you when you need it most.
- Show appreciation for their efforts to support and encourage you. Remember, your test may test the patience of everyone involved.

STUDY GROUPS

There's not necessarily any reason to study alone. If you're taking a test, then others are, too. Studying with one or more people can give you the motivation, support, and fresh perspective you need at such times.

Choose your study group members with care. If you are lucky enough to know other test takers well, then you can pick people whom you respect. You can meet with people you already know from your class or within your community, or you can post notices on a school bulletin board to reach others whom you don't know but who may be seeking this kind of support for a big test.

You may want to start your study group informally. Get together with a few people who are taking the same test. Talk with them to get a feel for how motivated they are and how they want to study together. If you don't feel comfortable with some or all of the group, you haven't made a commitment or wasted your time. If the group seems to be compatible, you can arrange for other meetings.

Pros and Cons of a Study Group

There are several advantages to working in a study group:

- You have the benefit of the notes, insights, and ideas of other people.
- Listening to the ideas of other people helps to clarify information for you.
- Study group members can offer support and encouragement to one another.

There are also some drawbacks to working in a study group:

- Sometimes, when people get together, they spend more time socializing than studying.
- Some group members may be competitive and not be willing to share information or resources with others.
- Some group members may tend to slack off and not take test preparation seriously, which can mean that they wind up not doing their share of group work.

Organizing a Study Group

How you choose people and structure the group can make all the difference in its ultimate success. One question you may consider at the outset is whether to study with friends or with strangers. There are benefits with and drawbacks to each choice. Some people feel more comfortable with friends or people they know well. They feel less competitive, perhaps, and are more willing to ask questions or share information with people with whom they have some prior association. On the other hand, groups that are too chummy may be groups that spend too much time socializing. This fact is why some people prefer a more businesslike or arms-length relationship with their "study buddies." They feel more comfortable with other students they do not know outside the classroom because they waste less time on personal conversation and spend more time on reviewing important material. Of course, groups made up of strangers lack the supportive feeling of a closer group, but they may also be more efficient by making better use of limited time.

Regardless of whether your group consists of friends or strangers, here are some tips to help your group succeed:

- Keep it small; three to six people are best. Larger groups are harder to manage.
- Appoint one person to be the contact person to arrange sessions.
- Have your study group meet in as neutral a place as possible. An ideal location for a study group in is a classroom after scheduled classes. Many libraries also have study rooms that will accommodate a few people who want to work together without disturbing others with their talk.
- Start each group session by creating an agenda or list of topics the group will discuss. Always decide at the beginning of each session how long you will work.
- Ask everyone to come to the meeting prepared with notes, questions, and patience.

SETTING YOUR SIGHTS

An important part of implementing any study plan is organizing that plan so it accomplishes a specific goal. In your case, it is probably to get a top grade. That overall goal, however, is best accomplished by setting and meeting a series of shorter goals that all lead to a high test score.

The study plan, as you recall, has four basic steps:

1. Set a time frame.
2. Make sure you have the correct information about the test.
3. Gather all your classroom and test-preparation materials together.
4. Stay on your plan and reward yourself for it.

Think of each one of these steps as a goal that will get you closer and finally take you to your ultimate goal. Then think of the time you need to accomplish these goals.

TIMING TRICKS

All the plans in the world won't help, of course, if you don't find time to actually study what you need to pass the test. You have to find the time to put your plan into action.

Making Your Plan Fit You

Here are some strategies for testing your plan against what you know about your personal time patterns and commitments:

- **Figure out what time you have available to study in a typical week.** Write down what you do on one typical school day and one typical weekend day.
- **Notice what hours seem to be free for study.** Are most of those hours in the evenings? In the daytime? How *many* hours are available for study? Is your study time in blocks (Wednesday afternoons and Saturday mornings, for example)? Or is your study time

in bits and pieces during the week (an hour each morning and half an hour late in the afternoon before the bus comes)?

- **Determine your own patterns.** Are you a morning person who can get up an hour early and study before breakfast? Are you a night owl who can work after everyone else is asleep? Are you accustomed to exercising regularly? Does exercise tire or energize you?

Answering these questions will help you choose the times that are best for you to study for your test. Once you've answered the questions, consider how your time frame fits the study plan you've devised by completing the weekly timetable at the end of this chapter.

Sticking to Your Plan

Now that you have a plan that will work, here are some strategies for sticking to it:

- **Write down your study schedule.** Post a copy where it will remind you of the times you need to study.
- **Don't abandon your study plan if you get off-track for a few days.** It's easy to become discouraged when outside events, family responsibilities, or personal problems keep you from your studies during the time you have scheduled for studying. Just pick up where you left off. Try to add a little time to two or three study sessions rather than trying to make up for lost study time by cramming or by skipping important material.
- **Adjust your study plan to meet changing needs.** For example, if you find that you need to do more practice tests than you had planned to do, take more time to do them. If you find that you are doing well on specific sections of the practice tests and less well on others, take more time on those sections that need your attention.

Remember that the purpose of the study plan is to organize your study time, not to dictate how to run your life or to make you feel guilty.

Now it's time to create your own weekly timetable on page 29 that incorporates all your responsibilities, including study time. If you're not sure what to include, take a look at the completed sample at the end of this chapter.

IN SHORT

You need to create a study plan to schedule your time leading up to a test. You can successfully carry out your study plan by finding a quiet location to study in, using adequate reading light, turning off the television and radio, asking your family and friends for help, and organizing a study group. Setting your study goals and writing down your study schedule will help you to master the material on your test.

WEEKLY TIMETABLE

On the following timetable for a week, cross out any hours during which you are occupied with family, recreation, meals, and any activities you do on a regular basis—team sports, community work, volunteer work, and so on. See what hours you have "free" to study.

	Sunday	Monday	Tuesday	Wednesday	Thursday	Friday	Saturday
6:00							
7:00							
8:00							
9:00							
10:00							
11:00							
12:00							
1:00							
2:00							
3:00							
4:00							
5:00							
6:00							
7:00							
8:00							
9:00							
10:00							
11:00							
12:00							

WEEKLY TIMETABLE

(Completed sample)

	Sunday	Monday	Tuesday	Wednesday	Thursday	Friday	Saturday
6:00							
7:00							
8:00							
9:00							
10:00							
11:00							
12:00	←		LUNCH			→	TENNIS PRACTICE
1:00							
2:00							
3:00							
4:00							
5:00		DINNER					
6:00							
7:00							
8:00						RECREATION	
9:00							
10:00							
11:00							
12:00							

3

Learning Strategies

How successful you are at studying has less to do with how much time you put in to it than with *how* you do it. That's because some ways of studying are much more effective than others, and some environments are much more conducive to studying than others. Another reason is that not everyone retains information in the same way.

▶ LEARNING STYLES

Think for a minute about what you know about how you learn. You've lived long enough to have a good feel for how you learn what you need to learn. For example, if you need directions to a new restaurant, would you:

- Ask to see a map showing how to get there?
- Ask someone to tell you how to get there?
- Copy someone's written directions?

Most people learn in a variety of ways: seeing, touching, hearing, and experiencing the world around them. Many people find, however, that they naturally tend to get information better from one learning source than others. The source that works best for you is called your dominant *learning modality*.

There are three basic learning modalities: the visual, the auditory, and the kinesthetic (also known as *tactile*).

- **Visual learners** understand and retain information best when they can *see* the map, the picture, the text, the word, or the math example.
- **Auditory learners** learn best when they can *hear* the directions, the poem, the math theorem, or the spelling of a word.
- **Kinesthetic learners** need to *write* the directions, *draw* the diagram, or *copy* down the phone number.

VISUAL LEARNERS

If you are a visual learner, you learn best by seeing. Pay special attention to illustrations and graphic material when you study. Color-code your notes with colorful inks or highlighters. Learn to map or diagram information (later in this chapter).

AUDITORY LEARNERS

If you are an auditory learner, you learn best by listening. Read material aloud to yourself, or talk about what you are learning with a study partner or a study group. Hearing the information will help you to remember it. Some people like to tape-record notes and play them back on the tape player.

KINESTHETIC LEARNERS

If you are a kinesthetic learner, you learn best by doing. Interact a lot with your print material by underlining and making margin notes in your textbooks and handouts. Rewrite your notes onto index cards. Recopying material helps you to remember it.

▶ How to Study Most Effectively

If studying efficiently and effectively is second nature to you, you're a rare bird indeed. Most people have to work at it. Here are some helpful study methods.

MAKING AN X-RAY

After you collect all the materials you need to review or prepare for the test, the first step for studying any subject is to reduce a large body of information into smaller, more manageable units. One approach to studying this way is to *X-ray* text information, handout material, and class notes.

Think about an X-ray. It is a picture of the bare bones of a body. The important information in print material is often surrounded by lots of extra words and ideas. If you can highlight just the important information, or at least the information you need for your test, you can help yourself narrow your focus so you can study more effectively. There are several ways to make X-ray pictures of print material. They include annotating, outlining, and mapping.

Annotating

Annotation means that you underline or highlight important information that appears in print material. It also involves responding to the material by engaging the writer in "conversation" by means of margin notes. Margin notes are phrases or sentences in the margins of print material that summarize the content of those passages.

> **Annotate with Restraint**
> Annotation should be thoughtful and selective. Underlining everything in the text prevents the "skeleton" of the text from being seen.

- Annotations pull out main ideas from the surrounding text and make them more visible and accessible.
- Margin notes leave footprints to follow in a review of the text.

Here is an example of a passage from Chapter 2 that has been annotated and underlined.

LOCATION, LOCATION, LOCATION

Find a quiet spot, use a good reading light, and turn the TV and radio off.

Find Quiet Places

Your quiet spot may be in a different place at different times of the day. For example, it could be the kitchen table early in the morning before breakfast, your school library, or a corner of the sofa late at night. If that's the case, make sure your study material is portable. Keep a folder or bag that contains your notes, practice tests, pencils, and other supplies. Then you can carry your study material with you throughout the day and study in whatever quiet spot presents itself.

Different quiet places at different times

Bag for study materials

If quiet study areas are nonexistent in your home, you may need to find a space elsewhere. The public library is the most obvious choice. Some test takers find it helpful to assign themselves study hours at the library in the same way that they schedule dentist appointments, class hours, household tasks, or other necessary uses of daily or weekly time. Studying away from home also minimizes the distractions of other people and other demands when you are preparing for a test.

Library!

Lights

Libraries also provide good reading lights. For some people this may seem like a trivial matter, but the eye strain that can come from working for long periods in poor light can be very tiring—a cause of fatigue you can't afford when you're studying hard. At home, the bedside lamp, the semidarkness of a room dominated by the television, or the bright sunlight of the back porch will be of little help to tired eyes.

Outlining

You are probably familiar with the basic format of the traditional outline:

I.   Main idea 1
    A. Major detail 1
    B. Major detail 2
        1. Minor detail 1
        2. Minor detail 2
II. Main idea 2
    A. Major detail 1
    B. Major detail 2

You may have used an outline to help you organize a writing assignment. Many writers outline their work before they begin to write.

When you outline print material, you're doing just the reverse: You're looking for the outline of the idea that has been buried in the text. When you are taking out the important information for a test, then you are looking for the X-ray of what the author wanted you to know.

Here's how you could outline the main ideas in Chapter 2 of this book, "Making and Carrying Out a Study Plan":

I.   Places to study
    A. Home
    B. Library
        1. Light
        2. Quiet

II. Who to study with
    A. Family
    B. Study group
        1. Advantages
        2. Disadvantages

Mapping

Mapping is a more visual kind of outline. Instead of a making a linear outline of the main ideas of a text, when you map, you make a diagram of the main points in the text that you want to remember. Again, using the text from Chapter 2, this diagram shows the same information in a map.

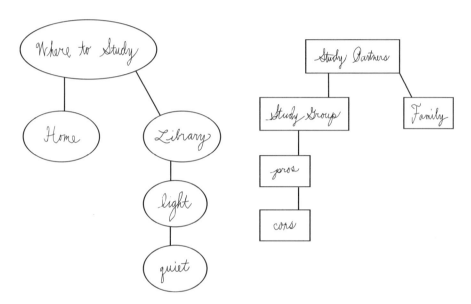

The point of all three of these strategies is that they allow you to pull out the most important information that you need to prepare for the test.

MAKE STUDY NOTES

The next step after you have pulled out all the key ideas is to make notes from which you will study.

You will use study notes for the intensive and ongoing study you'll do over a period of time before the test. They're the specific items that you targeted as important to know for the test and the tools by which you will learn to understand that information and, in many cases, commit to memory.

What kind of information do you put in study notes?

- The main ideas you underlined or highlighted in the text

- The main ideas and important details you outlined or mapped from the text
- Specific terms, words, dates, formulas, names, facts, or procedures that you need to memorize

How Do You Make Study Notes?

Some people like to write study notes in the back pages of their notebooks or on a paper folded lengthwise so that it can be tucked between the pages of a text or review book. This format is good to use for notes that can be written in two columns, such as questions and answers, causes and effects, or definition and examples.

Using Index Cards

Most study notes, especially those that contain material to be memorized, should be written on index cards.

There are a few advantages to making notes on index cards:

- The information on each card is visually separated from other information. This allows you to concentrate on just that one item, separate from the surrounding text. You remember the look of a vocabulary word or a math equation more clearly when it is set off by itself.
- Cards are small and portable. They can be carried in a purse or a pocket and pulled out at different times during the day for review, without the bulk and inconvenience of a book or notebook.

MAKING MEMORIZING EASIER

There are many ways to take the drudgery out of memorizing information.

Take Short Bites of Time

Most people memorize information best when they study in small periods over a long period of time. This is called *distributed practice.*

Memorizing facts from index cards that can be pulled out for a few ten-minute sessions each day will yield better results than sitting down with a textbook for an hour straight. Index card notes can be pulled out in seemingly unlikely moments: the ten minutes you are sitting in the car on your way to baseball practice, the eight minutes you spend waiting for class to start, or a quiet 15 minutes on the bus.

You'll find that these short but regular practices will greatly aid your recall of lots of information. It's an easy and painless way to add more study time to your schedule.

Break It Up

When you have a list to memorize, break the list into groups of seven or any other odd number. People seem to remember best when they divide long lists into shorter ones—and, for some reason, shorter ones that have an odd number of items in them! So instead of trying to memorize ten vocabulary or spelling words, split your list into smaller lists of seven and three, or five and five, to help you remember them.

Make Associations

You memorize best when you can attach meaning to what you are learning. In order to do this, you need to make associations with the material by *translating* the information into a practical example you can imagine in your own life. If you need to memorize the value of pi (π), which is 3.14, you may remember it better if you can make an association: we will have pie for my sister's birthday on 3/14.

Create Visual Aids

Give yourself visual assistance in memorizing. If there's a tricky combination of letters in a word you need to spell, for example, circle or underline it in red or highlight it in the text. Your eye will recall what the word looks like.

Do It Out Loud

Give yourself auditory assistance in memorizing. Many people learn best if they hear the information. Sit by yourself in a quiet room, and say aloud what you need to learn. Give your notes to someone else, and have that person ask you questions that you answer aloud.

Use Mnemonics

Mnemonics, or memory tricks, are used to help you remember what you need to know.

The most common type of mnemonic is the *acronym* (a word created from the first letters in a series of words). One acronym you may already know is HOMES, for the names of the Great Lakes (Huron, Ontario, Michigan, Erie, and Superior). ROY G BIV reminds people of the colors in the spectrum (red, orange, yellow, green, blue, indigo, and violet).

Another kind of mnemonic is a silly sentence made out of words that each begin with the letter or letters that start each item in a series. You may remember *Please Excuse My Dear Aunt Sally* as a sentence for remembering the order of operations in math (parentheses, exponents, multiply, divide, add, and subtract).

One of the oldest mnemonics that is still in use today is called the *method of loci*, which was first recorded more than 2,500 years ago. This technique was used by ancient orators to remember speeches, and it combines the use of organization, visual memory, and association. Today, it is often called the *place method*. The first step in using the place method is to think about a place you know very well, perhaps your living room or bedroom. Think of a location that has several pieces of furniture or other large items that always remain in the same place. These items become your *landmarks* or *anchors* in the place method mnemonic. The number of landmarks you choose will depend on the number of things you want to remember.

You need to know where each landmark is in the room, and when you visualize walking around this room, you must always walk in the same direction (an easy way to be consistent is to always move around the room in a clockwise direction or from the door to the opposite wall). What is essential is that you have a vivid visual memory of the path and objects along it.

The next step is to assign an item that you want to memorize to each landmark in your room. An effective technique is to visualize each word literally attached to each landmark. Here's an example of how one physical education student used the place method to remember the nine positions in baseball. This example uses landmarks in the student's bedroom.

PLACE METHOD SAMPLE

Landmark Positions

Landmark		Position
1. doorway	→ 1.	pitcher
2. chair	→ 2.	catcher
3. TV stand	→ 3.	first baseman
4. vase with flowers	→ 4.	second baseman
5. nightstand	→ 5.	third baseman
6. bed	→ 6.	shortstop
7. closet	→ 7.	left fielder
8. bookcase	→ 8.	center fielder
9. table with skirt	→ 9.	right fielder

Our student may imagine each baseball position written on or attached to each landmark. Or imagine each player connected to each landmark in some way: The pitcher is blocking the doorway, chewing gum and tossing the ball into his glove, and the second baseman is holding the flower vase with a number 2 on it.

To make the place method work, you must first study and understand each item you want to remember, so you can visualize it and directly link it to the right anchor in you chosen place. The more vivid—even bizarre—your visualization is, the stronger the connection will be between the material and the landmarks that are already entrenched in your memory.

Sleep on It

No one has yet figured out a way that people can just put the book under the pillow and wake up the next morning with its contents stashed neatly in their brains. But it is true that when you study right before sleep and don't allow any interference—such as conversation, radio, television, or music—to come between study and sleep, there is better recall of material. This is especially true if you review first thing after waking as well. A rested and relaxed brain seems to hang on to information better than a tired and stressed-out brain.

Sleep in Your Bed—Don't Study in It

You may think it makes sense, after a long day, to take a shower and get ready for bed so that you can read the chapter, memorize the vocabulary, and take the review test in comfort. Unfortunately, this is the quickest way to send yourself straight to sleep. You are out of study mode the minute you hit that mattress.

It certainly makes sense to find a place to study that is comfortable. And sometimes a shower can wake you up and make you feel refreshed. But your bed is probably too comfortable to be useful.

If you want to make reading in bed of some use to test preparation, don't try to seriously study in bed. Rather, use that time to read newspapers, magazines, and books that will make you well-informed on a variety of subjects. Even tests that are geared to skills, rather than facts, will often ask you about information that you may have learned through your reading. The more general knowledge you have, the more you bring to the testing room.

On page 41, there are exercises on annotating, mnemonics, mapping, and study card writing. After you complete the exercises, check out how you did by looking at the suggested answers that follow.

IN SHORT

You can learn to study more effectively for any test by creating an X-ray of the material you need to know. If you annotate, outline, and map study notes, the material will be easier for you to review. Studying in short bites of time, breaking up long lists of memory work into shorter ones, making associations, and creating mnemonics will help you learn the test material efficiently and effectively.

ANNOTATION

Following is a passage from this chapter to underline and annotate. Make margin summaries of the key points in each paragraph. Then make a mnemonic based on your margin notes.

Take Short Bites of Time

Most people memorize information best when they study in small periods over a long period of time. This is called *distributed practice*.

Memorizing facts from index cards that can be pulled out for a few ten-minute sessions each day will yield better results than sitting down with a textbook for an hour straight. Index card notes can be pulled out in seemingly unlikely moments: the ten minutes you are sitting in the car on your way to baseball practice, the eight minutes you spend waiting for class to start, or a quiet 15 minutes on the bus.

You'll find that these short but regular practices will greatly aid your recall of lots of information. It's an easy and painless way to add more study time to your schedule.

Break It Up

When you have a list to memorize, break the list into groups of seven or any other odd number. People seem to remember best when they divide long lists into shorter ones—and, for some reason, shorter ones that have an odd number of items in them! So instead of trying to memorize ten vocabulary or spelling words, split your list into smaller lists of seven and three, or five and five, to help you remember them.

Make Associations

You memorize best when you can attach meaning to what you are learning. In order to do this, you need to make associations with the material by *translating* the information into a practical example you can imagine in your own life. If you need to memorized the value of pi (π), which is 3.14, you may remember it better if you can make an association: we will have pie for my sister's birthday on 3/14.

Create Visual Aids

Give yourself visual assistance in memorizing. If there's a tricky combination of letters in a word you need to spell, for example, circle or underline it in red or highlight it in the text. Your eye will recall what the word looks like.

Do It Out Loud

Give yourself auditory assistance in memorizing. Many people learn best if they hear the information. Sit by yourself in a quiet room, and say aloud what you need to learn. Give your notes to someone else, and have that person ask you questions that you answer aloud. Tape record your notes and play them back to yourself at home or in the car.

Use Mnemonics

Mnemonics, or memory tricks, are used to help you remember what you need to know.

The most common type of mnemonic is the *acronym* (a word created from the first letters in a series of words). One acronym you may already know is HOMES, for the names of the Great Lakes (Huron, Ontario, Michigan, Erie and Superior). ROY G BIV reminds people of the colors in the spectrum (red, orange, yellow, green, blue, indigo, and violet).

Flash Cards

Make flash cards with definitions for each kind of learning modality:

- Visual
- Auditory
- Kinesthetic

Mapping

Following is an outline of the learning strategies covered in this chapter. Using the same information, make a map, or diagram, of the same material.

I. How to X-ray a text
   A. Annotating
   B. Outlining
   C. Mapping
II. How to make study notes
   A. Notebook pages
   B. Index cards
      1. Reasons for using index cards
III. Memory methods

(Completed sample)

ANNOTATION

Take Short Bites of Time

Most people memorize information best when they <u>study in small periods over a long period of time. This is called *distributed practice.*</u>

    Memorizing facts from index cards that can be pulled out for a few ten-minute sessions each day will yield better results than sitting down with a textbook for an hour straight. Index card notes can be pulled out in seemingly unlikely moments: the ten minutes you are on your way to baseball practice, the eight minutes you spend waiting for class to start, or a quiet 15 minutes on the bus.

    You'll find that these short but regular practices will greatly aid your recall of lots of information. It's an easy and painless way to add more study time to your schedule.

Distributed practice

Break It Up

When you have a list to memorize, <u>break the list into groups of seven or any other odd number.</u> People seem to remember best when they divide long lists into shorter ones—and, for some reason, shorter ones that have an odd number of items in them! So instead of trying to memorize ten vocabulary or spelling words, split your list into smaller lists of seven and three, or five and five, to help you remember them.

Divide lists

Make Associations

You memorize best when you can attach meaning to what you are learning. In order to do this, you need to make associations with the material by <u>*translating* the information into a practical example you can imagine in your own life.</u> If you need to memorized the value of pi (π), which is 3.14, you may remember it better if you can make an association: we will have pie for my sister's birthday on 3/14.

Translate

Create Visual Aids

Visual Aid

<u>Give yourself visual assistance in memorizing.</u> If there's a tricky combination of letters in a word you need to spell, for example, circle or underline it in red or highlight it in the text. Your eye will recall what the word looks like.

Do It Out Loud

Auditory

<u>Give yourself auditory assistance in memorizing.</u> Many people learn best if they hear the information. Sit by yourself in a quiet room, and say aloud what you need to learn. Give your notes to someone else, and have that person ask you questions that you answer aloud. Tape record your notes and play them back to yourself at home or in the car.

Use Mnemonics

Mnemonics, or memory tricks, are used to help you remember what you need to know.

Acronym

The most common type of mnemonic is the *acronym* (a word created from the first letters in a series of words). One acronym you may already know is HOMES, for the names of the Great Lakes (Huron, Ontario, Michigan, Erie and Superior). ROY G BIV reminds people of the colors in the spectrum (red, orange, yellow, green, blue, indigo, and violet).

Sample Mnemonic: DADVAT

Flash Cards

Here are samples of how your flash cards may look:

Visual modality— learning by seeing	Auditory modality— learning by listening	Kinesthetic modality— learning by touching or moving

Mapping

Here is an example of how your map or diagram may look:

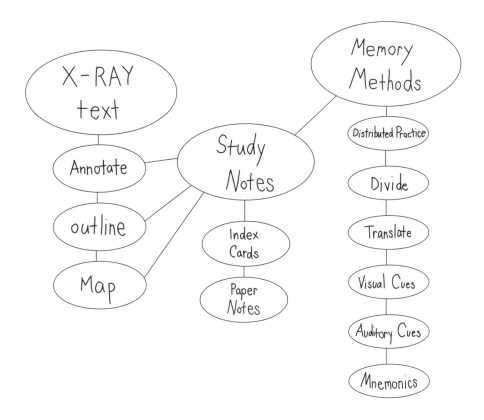

YOU CAN FIND AN ANSWER ONLY WHEN YOU HAVE A QUESTION.
ONCE YOU'VE IDENTIFIED WHAT YOU ALREADY KNOW IN YOUR
STUDY MATERIAL, YOU CAN FIND OUT WHAT YOU DON'T KNOW.
THEN YOU CAN CREATE QUESTIONS AND LOOK FOR THE
ANSWERS. AND THEN, YOU'LL HAVE LEARNED SOMETHING!

Knowing When You Don't Know

How often have you heard someone say, "I don't know"? That phrase is the key to studying. What separates experienced students from inexperienced ones is awareness of what they know and what they don't know. Those with academic experience know enough to ask the specific questions that will help them find the answers. Once they've found those answers, they've learned something new.

Separating Known from Unknown

George was studying geometry. "I know the answer!" he exclaimed when Abe asked him to work on a problem with him. "How do you know it?" Abe asked. "Well, I know what an equilateral triangle is because I see the word *equal* in it. That clues me to the fact that an equilateral triangle is a triangle with three equal sides."

"I know that, too," Abe said, "but I still don't know how to find the area of the equilateral triangle."

"Oh, you're right; I don't either," George said, looking at the problem again. "I jumped ahead too quickly; I recognized only what I knew about the problem, not what I didn't know. Let's look at this together. Maybe we can find something else we know that will help solve the problem."

▶ FINDING OUT WHAT YOU DO AND DON'T KNOW

After each study session, and after each class or lecture you attend, your final step must be to reflect on what you learned in that session or class. Thinking about the session lets you check what you know for sure and what you don't know.

The writer of your textbook, or the lecturer in your class, is taking you on a trip to some place you've never been before, and that "place" is a new piece of knowledge or a new set of facts. When the trip is over—when you've read the chapter or heard the lecture—you need to ask yourself the following questions:

- Where was the writer or teacher trying to take me? That is, what was the main idea of this reading or lecture?
- How did I get there? What were the steps that led to this main idea?
- Have I arrived? Do I understand this main idea and all the steps that led up to it?

The problem is that sometimes you can think you know more than you do. That is why it's important to *draw* your picture and *write* down the order. When you come to the point that you can't proceed with your drawing or list, you've hit the point when you should start asking questions.

Another way to find out what you know and what you don't is to role-play. Pretend you are the writer of your textbook, or your teacher. If you have a study buddy, one of you can be the writer or teacher and the other the student. Explain to your study buddy what you just read or heard. If you don't have a study buddy, explain it to yourself. Make sure you don't leave out any steps!

When you come to any point where your explanation is unclear, when it may not make sense to another person, you've found out what you don't know. That's when it's time to start asking questions. Once you have questions, you can find the answers, and then you will know something that you didn't know before.

▶ THE QUEST IS ON!

Finding what you know and then finding what you don't know is something you already know how to do. If you were in an unfamiliar town and wanted to get to Adams Street, you would know that you don't know how to get there, and you would ask directions.

Those directions would be based on what you already know—your location at the time. You're in the park, and you've been told Adams Street is near the park, but you don't know which direction to go. So you ask. And someone tells you to walk north until you get to the end of the park and then turn left and walk one block to Adams Street.

You may have one more question: Which way is north? And if you get an answer, you'd follow those directions, walking to the end of the park and turning left. So then you get to a street, but it doesn't have a street sign. How do you know if you've arrived? You stop someone passing by and ask again.

ASKING QUESTIONS, GETTING ANSWERS

The process of asking questions to find out, first, what you already know, and second, what you still need to learn, is similar. You may have to ask more than one question as you find your way to the knowledge the writer is trying to give you. Here's a sequence you can go through to find out what you don't know and then ask questions and get answers. If you have been reading a book, the text you'll go back to for answers is the book; if you listened to a lecture, your "text" is your notes or audiotape of the lecture.

1. Draw a picture and write down the order.
2. Is this perfectly clear? Where are the gaps?
3. Ask yourself a question that will help fill in the gap.
4. Go back to your text to find the answer. Use the parts of your picture or outline that are clear to help you see where in the text you should look for the answer. Look in the sections of your text that come right after the last clear piece of your picture or outline.
5. Read the relevant part of the text. Don't try to reread the whole chapter or go over the whole lecture; you're just looking for one little piece of information, the answer to your question. Take it in small chunks.

6. If you don't have an answer, reread the same section to try again.
7. If you still don't have an answer, read the parts that come just before and just after what you were reading. Repeat this process until you find the answer to your question.
8. Put this new piece of information into your picture and order. Is the picture clear now? Is the order clear?
9. Keep going back and forth between your study aids and the text until your picture and order are perfectly clear, and you have no questions left.

Now you've really learned something! You have a clear picture of the main idea, and you know all the steps it takes to get there. But notice that this clear picture and order don't come out all at once. You have to take it one step at a time, just as if you were following the directions to Adams Street. And you're always using what you know to help you find the answers to what you don't know.

Here's an example of how you use what you know to help you create questions: Suppose you had to fill in the blank in the following sentence:

When you don't know something, your brain rushes to _____e it has stored ideas on a similar topic.

In order to figure out what word should go in the blank, you should go through the following process:

First, ask yourself, "What do I know for sure about the sentence?" Your responses may be:

- I know that the sentence is about recognizing when I don't know something.
- I know that it's about the brain moving in some way.
- I know that there's a storing place in my brain.
- I know that the missing word connects the brain moving to the storage place.
- I know that the missing word ends with *e*.

Then, ask yourself, "What kind of word would connect the brain rushing and the storage place?" The word must have something to do with direction. You make up more questions by connecting the words you know that have to do with direction to the sentence:

- Is the word *over*? Over doesn't end with the letter *e*.
- Is it *here*? That's a direction word that ends in *e*, but *here* doesn't make sense in this sentence. Filling in that word doesn't give you a clear picture and a clear sense of order.
- You reject *there* for the same reason. The only word that really works in the sentence—that gives a clear picture and order—is *where*.

This was a simple example, but it shows you how to use what you already know to arrive at the answers to the questions about what you don't know.

Choose one paragraph from a book you are studying now. Write down the following in your notebook, or read it into your tape recorder:

- Identify what you know for sure by drawing a picture and writing down the order.
- Find what you don't know.
- Ask questions.
- Go through the steps previously listed to find the answers.
- Write or record additional questions as they come to mind.

IT'S ALL YOURS

The questions that count most are *your* questions. You get more out of studying; you become more involved, and enjoy it more; and it "sticks" more, when you make:

- Your own observations of what you know.
- Your own connections of new material to old.
- Your own questions and then find your own answers.

Often, the search for answers leads to more questions. And the more questions you ask, the clearer you're making your answers.

YOU'RE IN COMMAND!

You're taking control of your own learning when you:

- Recognize what you know.
- Recognize what you don't know.
- Create questions to make the pictures in your head and the order of events clear.
- Discover answers to your questions.
- Realize when and how to question what you've studied.

HOW TO ASK QUESTIONS, DEPENDING ON YOUR LEARNING STYLE

The most effective ways to ask questions are different for people with different learning styles.

- **If you learn best by seeing:** Write or draw what you know, and what questions you have.

- **If you learn best by hearing:** Read aloud as you write, and/or use a tape recorder.
- **If you learn best by images:** Draw or describe the pictures and/or maps in your head. Focus on when the pictures are *un*clear. Ask questions to clear your pictures.
- **If you learn best by order:** Make a list and/or timeline—focus on what is unclear; ask questions to develop a clearer order.
- **If you learn best by doing:** Imagine yourself experiencing what you're studying. Focus on when the experience feels unclear; ask questions to make the experience clearer, more real.

IN SHORT

You need to know what you *do* know in order to find what you *don't* know. Reflect on what you've studied. Thinking about what you've read or listened to lets you find what you know for sure and what you don't. Ask yourself questions so the picture in your head is clear, and the events are in an order that makes sense to you.

YOU CAN MAKE MORE SENSE OF WHAT YOU'RE READING WHEN YOU GET INVOLVED WITH IT. AND YOU CAN DO THIS BY ANTICIPATING WHAT YOU READ BEFORE YOU BEGIN. WHILE YOU READ, ASK QUESTIONS, MAKE PICTURES IN YOUR HEAD, TAKE NOTES, AND USE YOUR LEARNING STYLES. STOP WHEN YOU DON'T KNOW SOMETHING, WAIT UNTIL YOU UNDERSTAND IT, AND THEN CONTINUE WITH THE READING. AFTER YOU'VE FINISHED READING, THINK ABOUT WHAT YOU'VE LEARNED.

Getting More Out of Reading

Here's a hard but not surprising truth: *Reading is work.* It can be easy and enjoyable work, like reading a good story or the comics. Or, it can be more challenging work, such as reading a textbook or other study material.

Now think a minute about an after-school job or activity you may have. If you show up and just sit there until it's time to go home, did you work? No, you put in your time, but you didn't work—and if you keep acting that way, your coworkers or teammates won't value you. It's the same way with reading. If you just sit there, moving your eyes over the page, you aren't really reading—and you're not getting anything out of it. To get the most out of, and remember, what you read, you have to get actively involved in the material. Your mind should be working before, while, and after you read.

> ### There's Reading—and There's Reading
>
> "I just don't get this marine biology book. I can't understand the first chapter. I read it, and I don't get anything out of it," Sally complains to Harry.
>
> "How are you reading it?" Harry asks.
>
> "What do you mean—how?" she answers.
>
> "Well, how involved are you with what you're reading?"
>
> "What do you mean—involved? Reading is like TV—you look at it and you get meaning," Sally says.
>
> "It sounds like you need to read more actively," Harry tells her. "Reading is very different from watching TV."
>
> Sally has a problem. She expects reading to come to her, like her favorite sitcom on TV. She's not treating reading as work, but rather as a relaxing pastime. Having a difficult reading assignment make sense means asking questions, making connections, and creating order—getting involved!

▶ BEFORE YOU READ

WHAT'S IN A TITLE?

You have a title, even if you didn't win a world heavyweight boxing match. *Mr., Ms., Mrs.,* and *Miss* are titles. In a sense, so are *Mom, Dad, Sis,* and *Brother.* And there are many more. Get out your notebook and list your own titles. Start with your name, your family relationships, and what people call you in a formal setting (like Mr. or Ms.). List your job titles and any positions you hold in volunteer or professional organizations.

Like people, chapters, lessons, and books have titles that tell you what they're about. Just as you know Ms. Smith isn't a man, you know the article "Cooking Peas" isn't about carrots. Titles eliminate confusion and give a general impression before the finer details are known. Titles can tell you a lot—don't overlook them!

Test the definition of *title* by applying it to the chapter you are reading now. The chapter title is "Getting More Out of Reading." Read the summary that appears next to the title. It says the same thing as the chapter title, but with more details. The chapter section you're reading now is called "What's in a Title?" It's part of a larger section called "Before You Read." As you make sense of what the author is saying about titles, you're answering the question of this section's title, "What's in a Title?"

GET READY TO READ

Start thinking about what you will be reading before you even begin to read. First, choose a section to read. If the reading is divided into chapters, a chapter is a good place to start. If it's a long chapter with subheadings, begin with the first subheading. Look at the *title* of the chapter, the subheading, or the article only. Write down your answers to these questions:

- What does the title make you think of?
- What do you expect the reading to be about?
- What questions do you expect the reading to answer?

If Sally, who we met in the beginning of this chapter, followed this advice, her mind wouldn't start to drift to other things, like what she's doing tonight or how she's going to get home. She would be actively engaged in deciphering titles in her marine biology book. Making a study plan and sticking to it would help Sally stop daydreaming.

USING ILLUSTRATIONS

If the reading has any illustrations, photographs, or drawings, look at those, too. Write:

- what the illustrations seem to be about
- how the illustrations may connect with the title

When you study the title and illustrations before you read, you are *pre-reading*. You are preparing to read by first getting in touch with what you already know about the topic.

USING YOUR OWN SPECIAL FILING SYSTEM

Your brain has a wonderful filing system. It files everything you have seen, heard, tasted, and felt. All your experiences are up there—both your actual experiences and what you learned through reading, seeing, and listening. Information is stored in different compartments of your brain; each compartment has a specialty.

When you pre-read, you are reminding yourself of information you already know. You're putting yourself right in front of the "file cabinet" you need, ready to pull other information you already know—and ready to add new information. When you pre-read, you are more likely to remember what you've read. You're also more likely to enjoy it because you've begun to connect it with what you already know.

Sally, the marine biology student, remembers her summer trips to the beach as a child. She remembers the different kinds of shells she collected. Her mental file cabinet is ready for new files on marine biology. She begins making sense of what she is reading—and to enjoy and learn from the marine biology book.

▶ As You Read

Now that you've already gotten into the file cabinet in your head by pre-reading, you want to be ready to add new folders or information to your file cabinet. You need to be able to hold onto the new information you'll acquire as you begin to read the article or chapter.

KEEPING A READING LOG

When you wrote down or recorded your pre-reading ideas and questions, you began your *reading log*. This is a notebook (or audiotape) that helps you keep track of what you're reading, what it means to you, what questions you have, and what answers you are discovering.

You add to it when you write and/or draw pictures to make sense of new information. It's a good idea to take notes on everything you read. You may want to use thin notebooks that you can easily carry anywhere you find yourself reading. Perhaps your instructor has test booklets you could use for reading logs. These can be folded into a pocket or purse, making it easy to read and take notes while you're just about anywhere—on the bus, in the cafeteria, or in a waiting room.

You may want to make a narrow column on each page of your reading log to jot down the page numbers of the text you're writing notes about. This makes it easy for you to go back to check information. If you're expected to write a report on what you read, your log provides you with a head start. In it, you've already written pages that refer to specific information, quotes of what's important or questionable, your feelings on what you read, questions that you had, and what associations and experiences came to mind.

You can also keep a reading log on audiotape, although this is a little less convenient. However, if you're strongly oriented to using your ears rather than your eyes, you may find that speaking into a tape and listening to it later is more useful than writing in a notebook. In that case, make sure you have a small tape recorder you can carry with you anywhere.

This reading log is just for you. No one else will ever see or hear it unless you choose to show it to someone. So you can write or say whatever you want. Even if the associations you make seem a little silly to you, even if your questions seem too stupid to ask in class—write them down. Those silly associations may help you remember, and those stupid questions can't be answered until you ask them, even of yourself.

EXPERIENCE COUNTS!

Every time you read something new, you're adding to your experience. To help you hold onto the new information, continue to connect it with what you already know. If something is new to you and you have little experience that relates to it, be prepared to stop. Stopping helps you remember and gives your brain time to process what you've just learned.

After you've read the first couple of sentences of a reading, ask yourself what it means and how it goes along with your pre-reading idea of what it was going to be about. Look for the main idea of the reading, which is usually found either in an introduction or first paragraph.

For example, Sally, who is studying marine biology, should stop and ask herself, "What was in that first paragraph that sticks out in my mind? Is this what I expected from reading the title and subheadings of this chapter?" If nothing stands out about the first paragraph or two, she should go back and read them again.

WHEN EXPERIENCE FAILS YOU

What about when there's little of your own experience to connect with the reading? You'll probably have trouble understanding. So stop. Take some time to go over the section that's giving you trouble. Use your reading log, reread the text, and use your learning style to help you understand.

Put It in Your Reading Log

If you're having trouble understanding something you're reading, start by writing about it or talking into your tape recorder. Ask yourself the following questions:

- What does this make me think of?
- What pictures come to mind?
- What is the most important word in the sentence?

Sally found the book's reference to a marine biology lab strange because she had never been in such a lab. She tried to pretend she was a marine biologist. She used her experience of being in her dentist's office. She thought of the different tools her dentist used, and she applied that to imagining what a marine biologist's office may be like. She decided it would be on a boat. Then she went back to the reading and focused on the word *laboratory*. She felt much more comfortable and secure now that she had formed a picture in her mind. She *knew* what she was reading.

If the text is yours to keep, circle important words, and draw a picture in the margin of what comes to mind. For now, skip over any words you don't know. This way, you'll keep your pace and hold onto the idea of what you're reading. If the text is not yours, use scratch paper or, better yet, your reading log.

Reread the Text

When a text has you stumped, what do you do? Read the text over again, looking for:

- images that are clear to you
- an order of events that is clear to you

Once you know which parts you understand, you have a key to help you with the parts you don't understand. Ask yourself, "What do I need to know to make the pictures and order clear?" Perhaps some answers will be found in a passage that comes before the section you're reading. Start with the part you do understand, and use information from the difficult section to add to your picture or order.

If more questions come to mind, read the text over again until you've discovered your answers. You're putting new material into the file cabinet in your head. Don't rush; it takes time.

Use Your Learning Style

Use your learning style or styles as you stop and become comfortable with the new material, thinking about what you just read or listened to. Your brain needs time to file what you're learning so you can pull out the file later when you need it for a test. Read aloud, draw pictures or cartoons, make a timeline—whatever works for you.

Go to a chapter you haven't seen yet in this book. Choose a paragraph toward the end of the chapter. Make sure you don't read what comes before the paragraph! Follow the suggestions above for pre-reading and beginning to read. Then read the paragraph, and write your observations and questions in your notebook.

▶ AFTER YOU'VE READ

Almost everyone can remember what came first and what came last better than they remember what was in the middle—be it a shopping list or scenes in a play. That's why writers and teachers generally put the nitty-gritty, the main idea, of what you're reading in the beginning, and repeat it at the end.

Every time you complete an assignment, think about what you got out of it. In your reading log, answer these questions:

- What was most useful or interesting about what you read?
- How did the beginning compare with the end?
- What did you disagree with or find confusing?
- What ways of reading worked best for you (reading aloud, drawing pictures, etc.)?

NOW YOU SEE IT, NOW YOU DON'T

Here's a secret to reading: Some words have two different kinds of meanings, literal and figurative. One meaning you can feel, see, hear, smell, or taste. It's really there. A second meaning you have to figure out, based on the first meaning.

For instance, think about the word *road*. Imagine the road near you. You can see it; when someone walks or drives on it, you can hear traffic on it; if it's a tar road and a warm day, you can even smell it. A word meaning something that's really there is called *literal*. If you're a literal (right-brain) learner, literal understanding generally comes readily to you.

Some words also have a symbolic or *abstract* meaning. With the example of *road*, what does a road *do*? It takes you somewhere, right? Now you see that you can use *road* in a different way, an abstract way, a way that does not have a picture—a way that is not literal. Because you have to figure out this kind of meaning, it is called *figurative*. Reading this book may be part of your "road to success." You're getting somewhere—you just can't literally see it. If you're an abstract (left-brain) thinker, this kind of thinking generally comes readily to you.

To get from a *literal* understanding of a word to its *figurative* meaning, try this:

- First, picture the literal meaning in your head.
- Next, write (or tape-record) a description of what the word does.
- Then, hold on to the *idea* of what the word does, and consider its figurative meanings.

Try this approach in going from a literal to figurative understanding with other words. Think about the word *chair*. What does a chair do? It supports you. Were you ever chair of a committee? Get the idea?

Try this with titles, too. What is the literal meaning of a title? What could a figurative meaning be? Notice the title of a film, short story, poem, or play. Often there are two meanings to fiction, one literal—one you can easily picture—and another figurative—one you need to figure out. For example, the film *The Freshman* is about a young man who is in his first year of college (literal) and who is also naive, inexperienced, and "fresh" to the ways of the world (figurative).

If English isn't your first language, be on the lookout for many words and phrases with figurative meanings. To say, "A bell went off in her head," doesn't mean she had an operation, a bell was placed inside her head, and it rang! Instead, ask yourself, What picture comes to mind? A bell ringing. What does a ringing bell signify? It may announce something or call attention to something, right? It brings something to mind that wasn't thought of before. "A bell went off inside her head" figuratively means "She realized something." You'll find that the more practice you have, the easier it will be to go from literal to figurative understanding—from "seeing" something to realizing its figurative, richer meaning!

IN SHORT

To make sense of what you read, first study the title and any illustrations to figure out with the main idea of the reading. Come up with questions that the text should answer. You want to have clear images in your head, and a clear sense of the order of events of what you're reading or listening to. Stop when you come to something new or confusing. Connect it with what you already know, to help your brain file it as something learned. After you read, you think back on what you read and how you read it.

Coping with Test Anxiety

Test anxiety is like the common cold. Most people suffer from it periodically. It won't kill you, but it can make life miserable for days. Like a cold, test anxiety (TA for short—let's give it a nickname, so it's more comfortable to talk about.) can vary in severity. Sometimes it's no more than a little sniffle of dread about an upcoming exam. Sometimes it's a full-blown attack of what feels like imminent death. There are people who seem to be more vulnerable to TA in general and suffer badly from it. Others are better able to cope with the symptoms and get over it quickly. The point is, some degree of TA is inevitable for most, so until there is a cure, you need to find ways to deal with the affliction.

▶ SYMPTOMS OF TEST ANXIETY

A mild case of TA may only feel like a few butterflies in your stomach as you head toward your testing room and a little shaking of the hands as the test is given out. Both symptoms subside as soon as you become absorbed in taking the test.

Actually, a little TA is beneficial. That slight adrenaline rush is energizing and stimulates concentration and attention to the task of test taking. Not to worry.

If you're stricken with a more severe bout of TA, you probably have persistent feelings of dread or fear, changes in your patterns of eating and sleeping, and occasional unusual mood swings. Some people fear that they will "freeze" while they are taking the test and be unable to perform successfully, even if they know the answers.

You need to worry about test anxiety only if it is extreme enough to impair your performance. The following questionnaire will provide a diagnosis of your level of test anxiety. In the blank before each statement, write the number that most accurately describes your experience.

0 = Never   1 = Once or twice   2 = Sometimes   3 = Often

_____ I have gotten so nervous before an exam that I put down the books and didn't study for it.

_____ I have experienced disabling physical symptoms such as vomiting and severe headaches because I was nervous about an exam.

_____ I have not shown up for an exam because I was scared to take it.

_____ I have experienced dizziness and disorientation while taking an exam.

_____ I have had trouble filling in the little circles because my hands were shaking too hard.

_____ I have failed an exam because I was too nervous to finish it.

_____ Total: Add up the number is the preceding blanks.

Here are the steps you should take, depending on your score. If you scored:

- **Less than 3,** your level of test anxiety is nothing to worry about; it's probably just enough to give you that little extra edge.
- **Between 3 and 6,** you test anxiety may be enough to impair your performance, and you should practice the stress management techniques listed in this section to try to bring your test anxiety down to manageable levels.
- **More than 6,** your level of test anxiety is a serious concern. In addition to practicing the stress management techniques listed in this section, you may want to seek additional personal help. Call your local high school or community college and ask for the academic counselor. Tell the counselor that you have a level of test anxiety that sometimes keeps you from being able to take the exam. The counselor may be willing to help you or may suggest someone else you should talk to.

▶ Help for Severe Test Anxiety

Intense, crippling TA is fairly uncommon, but when it strikes, it may actually make it impossible for some people to take tests that could be important to them. People who suffer from this condition are quite literally paralyzed with fear. They become overwhelmed by it, and the consequences are severe mental and physical distress that could include vomiting, fainting, weeping spells, and depression.

If you suffer stress of this kind, the kind that doesn't diminish with simple, practical management techniques, you should seek counseling before preparing yourself for an important exam.

▶ Causes of Test Anxiety

Why do people suffer from TA in the first place? Well, TA grows out of the fear of doing poorly on a test. Depending on what kind of test you have to take, those risks may include many different things.

Many concerns about testing are real, such as:

- failing an important course
- getting cut from a sports team
- not getting into the course, college, or program you want

In the midst of a TA attack, you may manage to make matters worse by adding less concrete but equally scary risks such as:

- disappointing yourself (*I always knew I was stupid!*)
- disappointing others (*What will my parents/teacher/friend think of me?*)
- facing an uncertain future (*What happens to me now?*)
- repeating the failure (*I can't take this all over again!*)

▶ Preventing Test Anxiety

As with most unhealthy conditions, the best cure for TA is prevention. The more you can ward off an attack of TA, the better you will do on your test. Here are some preventive measures:

- **Keep a well-organized routine in your life.** Try to minimize the small problems that clutter up your mental landscape. Keep in mind that most minor problems are resolved without major fanfare.
- **Reduce as much general stress as you can.** A stressed-out life is a fertile field for test anxiety.
- **See the good, smart, resourceful person in the mirror every day.** Any time you're ready to beat yourself up about something, remind yourself of something good about yourself. (*I don't believe I made that stupid comment. On the other hand, I'm glad I wrote that note to Jane. She really seemed to be touched by it.*)
- **Stay healthy.** This is one of the most important ways you can keep from being overtaken by worries and anxieties of any kind. Diet and exercise help create a sense of well-being that prevents the more severe forms of TA.

▶ TREATING TEST ANXIETY

Inevitably, despite all the preventive maintenance you do, you're bound to develop at least some of the signs of TA. Here are some suggestions for managing it when it strikes.

STEP #1: CONFRONT YOUR FEARS

Standing up to fear is the same as standing up to a bully who would rob you of your self-esteem and confidence. Confront your fears and refuse to be intimidated.

Put Your Fears on Paper

Think about the real and imagined risks of failure on your test. *Write them down.* They will seem much smaller on the page than they do in your head. Do this especially if you get into the habit of waking up in the middle of the night with your brain racing with imagined horrors of failure. Get up. Turn on the light. Take out a piece of paper. In two columns, write down the fear (now called the *problem*) and what to do about it (now called the *solution*). *Here's an example:*

Problem	Solution
I have to go to the family reunion this weekend. How will I find the time to stick to my study plan? What if I fall behind?	I'll take my index cards with me, and I'll find some short periods of time to review some vocabulary. I'll get my brother to quiz me in the car.

Think about the Worst That Could Happen

Another mind game to play is *worst case scenario*. Ask yourself what the very worst outcome of failure would be. Then ask yourself, "So what? Will the world come to an end? Will my mother stop loving me? Am I less of a person than I was before the test?"

Of course not. Perspective is very important to performance. It is necessary, of course, to be serious about success. But it is not necessary to lose sight of other important aspects of your life.

STEP #2: BE OVERLY PREPARED

Probably the best prescription for success when you take any test (and certainly the best medicine for TA) is being so prepared that the risks of failure almost disappear. This remedy goes beyond the mere limits of systematic study, however. It means to *over-learn* your material.

Over-learning is just what the word implies: learning the material so well that your answers to questions are practically automatic. An obvious example of over-learning for most people is the multiplication tables. They repeated them so often while in school that they can retrieve them without conscious thought.

Over-learning is accomplished in several ways. It isn't just a matter of adding to the number of hours you spend studying for your test. It means learning in a specifically active, self-directed way. To over-learn, use all of your senses:

- **Look** at the information.
- **Write** the information.
- **Talk** the information through with someone else so you can absorb it and relate to it.
- **Listen** to yourself and someone else talk about it.

Become so familiar with the material that you don't even have to hear all of the question before you say the answer.

STEP #3: EXCUSE YOURSELF FROM EXCUSES

When people do poorly at something or are afraid they might do poorly, they tend to find excuses for their failures. Some of these excuses seem to make a lot of sense and do contain some elements of truth:

- "I didn't have enough time to study because of school, family, and community demands on my time."
- "I got sick before the test and couldn't study."
- "I couldn't understand the teacher, the textbook, or the test."

- "I'm just no good at those tests anyway. No matter how hard I try, I just can't get a good grade, so why bother?"

The problem with excuses is that they don't take away the test anxiety. They make it worse by adding another layer of guilt and nerves to the process. Excuses take away your power over your own actions. You are reduced to being a victim of time/health/bad tests/bad teachers/bad luck. Accept the reality of possible sickness, heavy schedules, or difficult courses.

Another remedy for TA, then, is to take control over your own behavior in response to challenges. Take personal responsibility for your study, and you'll feel the grip of anxiety lessen.

STEP #4: VISUALIZE SUCCESS

One of the ways you can take charge of your behavior in the face of test anxiety, possibly worsened by excuses and guilt, is to imagine your way to success. This is done by visualizing.

The term *visualizing* may be familiar to you because it is used often these days by sports psychologists and trainers working with athletes and others who suffer from performance anxiety. These people are trained to envision the success toward which they are driven. A runner makes a mental picture of the goal line. The gymnast imagines the announcer reeling off a row of perfect scores following a competition: *ten, ten, ten, ten.*

You, too, can envision yourself seeing an *A* posted on the bulletin board next to your name, or the celebration at home after you pass that critical test. Keeping your mental eye on the prize that the test brings you is an effective—and pleasant—antidote to the stress of test anxiety.

STEP #5: BLOCK YOUR ESCAPES AND TAKE DOWN YOUR DEFENSES

Another way you can empower yourself to defeat TA is to overcome two common tendencies to escape the discomfort posed by the fear of failure. One escape route is through *procrastination.* The other is by means of *defense mechanisms.*

Procrastinating—deliberately or unconsciously delaying study until it's too late to succeed— is a good way to sabotage your own best efforts in preparing for a test. The more you procrastinate, the more guilt you feel. The guiltier you feel, the more you worry. The more you worry, the worse the outcome on the test.

Block that temptation to delay by making and sticking to your study plan. Put your review book or study notes out where you can't avoid them. Write notes to yourself and leave them on your mirror or pillow, in your lunch bag, or over the visor in your car. You can't run from yourself forever!

Another way you may try to defend yourself is by holding back from a real push to success because of a fear that your best isn't good enough. You feel better if you can say, "Well, if I'd had the time/health/ support/encouragement, I could have passed." It's discouraging to say, "I did my absolute best, and I still failed."

The problem is that you don't need the additional burden of discouragement on top of a bout with TA. Give it your best shot. After all, a good, solid try is still your best defense against failure.

IN SHORT

A slight case of test anxiety (TA) may help you concentrate on the test. However, a more severe case of TA can sabotage your success, so you should actively prevent or eliminate it. TA is caused by fear and can be prevented by staying organized, reducing other stress, staying healthy, and being positive. You can eliminate TA by confronting your fears, overlearning the test material, giving up excuses, visualizing success, and overcoming procrastination.

MANAGING YOUR TEST ANXIETY

Before you take a major classroom or standardized test that makes you anxious, write down answers to the following questions.

I want to do well on this test because

_____

_____

What is the worst thing that could happen if I fail this test?

_____

_____

(See? Your fears already look less scary when you see them written down.)

How would I handle it if I did do poorly on the test? What would I do?

_____

_____

Some things I could do to keep myself from suffering from test anxiety are

_____

_____

When I see myself doing well on this test, I picture

_____

_____

MANAGING YOUR TEST ANXIETY

(Completed sample)

I want to do well on this test because
I need to do well on the SAT.

What is the worst thing that could happen if I fail this test?
If I don't do well on the SAT, I might not get into the school of my choice.
(See? Your fears already look less scary when you see them
written down.)

How would I handle it if I did do poorly on the test? What would I do?
I would study harder and take the test again.

Some things I could do to keep myself from suffering from test anxiety are
work out, study one hour per day, and practice deep breathing.

When I see myself doing well on this test, I picture
handing in the test at the end with a big smile on my face.

IN THIS CHAPTER, YOU WILL LEARN HOW TO TACKLE THE MOST
COMMON TYPE OF EXAM QUESTION—THE MULTIPLE-CHOICE
QUESTION. THIS CHAPTER INTRODUCES THE MULTIPLE-CHOICE
FORMAT AND DEALS WITH QUESTIONS REQUIRING RECALL OR
RECOGNITION OF MATERIAL, READING A CHART OR GRAPH, AND
ANSWERING MATH QUESTIONS.

Psyching Out the Multiple-Choice Test

Test questions are geared to tap in to your knowledge of subject matter or to measure your skills at performing some task. Some test questions require you to *recall* specific items of information; others ask you only to *recognize* information by separating it from similar choices. And still others have you reason out answers based on text presented in the test itself. All of these kinds of questions are most frequently presented in a multiple-choice format in which you must choose the one best answer.

Generally speaking, multiple-choice questions are considered to be *objective* questions because they are based solely on the information; they don't allow for the opinion or interpretation of the test taker.

▶ WHY MULTIPLE CHOICE?

Multiple choice is the most popular format for most standardized tests for two reasons:

- Like most short-answer tests, they are easier and quicker to grade.
- They do not penalize test takers who know the information but have poorly developed writing skills or problems with expressive language.

► How the Questions are Written

You may remember taking tests that contained questions like this one:

1. The largest of the Great Lakes is
   a. Huron.
   b. Superior.
   c. Erie.
   d. Mississippi.

The answer is **b.** This is a much simpler example than you would find on the SAT or ACT, but it does contain the three elements of most multiple-choice questions, which are *stems*, *options*, and *distractors*.

Stem:	"The largest of the Great Lakes is"
Options:	All answer choices
Distractors:	Incorrect answer choices

STEMS

Stems contain the information on which the question is based. In longer tests, the stems of the questions may be as long as a paragraph and could contain a lot of information that you must sift through before you can choose an answer.

Sometimes stem questions are phrased as *situations*. Situation questions set a scene or set of facts on which the test taker is required to answer a series of questions. Stems can also be simply a word, a math example, or a fragment of a sentence that serves to frame the question.

OPTIONS

Options are the answer choices offered to you, the test taker. Many options require that you simply recognize a correct choice among several others.

2. As president, Ronald Reagan came to be known as
   a. Old Hickory.
   b. The Great Communicator.
   c. Speaker of the House.
   d. Old Ironsides.

The answer is **b.**

Some test makers test the accuracy of your knowledge by offering two or more options that are similar.

> **3.** The word in the following sentence that means the same or almost the same as *flammable* is
>   a. fireproof.
>   b. fire resistant.
>   c. easily burned.
>   d. burning.

It wouldn't be enough in this question that you know that *flammable* has something to do with fire. All of the options offer that choice. You have to know that the particular word pertaining to fire that you want means that something is easily burned, choice **c**.

DISTRACTORS

Distractors are the incorrect answers that offer a challenge to the test takers. In question 2, the distractors are choices **a**, **c**, and **d**; and in question 3, they are choices **a**, **b**, and **d**.

Distractors are often written to force test takers to be very careful in their selections. In question 2, for instance, if you didn't know that Reagan was known by the epithet *the Great Communicator*, you could be distracted by the two choices that refer to age. Because Reagan was one of our oldest presidents while in office, you may be tempted to choose one of them.

The wise test taker will eliminate the clearly impossible options first. In question 2, both *Old Ironsides*, which is the name of a ship, and *Speaker of the House*, which is an office that cannot be held by a sitting president, should be eliminated. Then, between *Old Hickory* and *the Great Communicator*, you would have to make a choice. If you remembered that *Old Hickory* was the term used to describe President Andrew Jackson, you would eliminate it, and then the correct choice would be obvious.

► RECOGNITION AND RECALL QUESTIONS

As noted before, multiple-choice questions force you to recall or recognize specific information that is surrounded by other similar but incorrect options. These other options can be written in such a way that they confuse the unwary or unwise test taker.

4. Choose the word or phrase that means the same or almost the same as the word *secession.*
  a. a meeting
  b. the act of breaking away from a political body
  c. a surgical birth
  d. a parade

5. Circle the word that is correctly spelled in the following group of words.
  a. chanel
  b. channel
  c. chanle
  d. chanell

6. Choose the correct punctuation from the following choices.
  I went to lunch with my two
  a. sister in laws.
  b. sister-in-laws.
  c. sister's in law.
  d. sisters-in-law.

  In questions 4 through 6, you would have to rely on your memory for the definition of *secession,* the spelling of the word *channel,* and the plural forms for hyphenated words, or you would have to be able to recognize the correct answer in comparison to the other choices. The correct answers are: 4 is choice **b**, 5 is choice **b**, and 6 is choice **d**. Some strategies for approaching these kinds of questions are outlined next.

LET YOUR EYE BE YOUR GUIDE
Look at the four choices of spelling. Which *looks* like something you've seen before? (*channel*)

LET YOUR EAR BE YOUR GUIDE
Listen to the differences between *sister-in-laws* and *sisters-in-law.* Which sounds better? (*sisters-in-law.*) You would have to remember the hyphen rule in this word, however.

Beware! Note distractors in choices **c** and **d** in question 4. Many multiple-choice questions are designed to confuse you by offering options that sound like the stem word or have associations with the stem word. In this instance, the similarity between *procession* and *secession,* and the distant but confusing sound similarities between *secession* and the medical shorthand *C-section* for *cesarean section* could trap the unwary test taker.

TRY EACH OPTION AS A TRUE/FALSE QUESTION

"A secession is a meeting. True or false?" "A secession is an act of breaking away from a political body. True or false?" Which statement seems to make the most sense?

▶ READING AND REASONING QUESTIONS

Some multiple-choice questions are geared to measure your ability to take information directly from the text and to answer questions based on that text. This format is used in the SAT and ACT. These kinds of multiple-choice questions typically measure reading comprehension.

Generally, reading comprehension tests start with a passage on a particular subject, followed by as few as two or as many as ten questions based on the content of that passage.

These questions usually are aimed at four skills:

1. Recognizing the *definition* of a vocabulary word in the passage
2. Identifying the *main idea* of the passage
3. Noting a specific *fact or detail* in the passage
4. Making an *inference or conclusion* based on information in the passage that is not directly stated

Read the following passage and the four questions that follow. Identify each type of question from the previous list.

> The "broken window" theory was originally developed to explain how minor acts of vandalism or disrespect can quickly escalate to crimes and attitudes that break down the entire social fabric of an area or unit. It is an idea that can easily be applied to any situation in society. The theory contends that if a broken window in an abandoned building is not replaced quickly, soon all the windows in that building will be broken.
>
> In other words, a small violation, if condoned, leads others to commit similar or greater violations. Thus, after all the windows have been broken, the building is likely to be looted and perhaps even burned down. According to this theory, violations increase exponentially. Thus, if disrespect to a superior

is tolerated, others will be tempted to be disrespectful as well. A management crisis could erupt literally overnight.

For example, if one firefighter begins to disregard proper housewatch procedure by neglecting to keep up the housewatch administrative journal, and this firefighter is not reprimanded, others will follow suit by committing similar violations of procedure, thinking, "If he can get away with it, why can't I?" So what starts out as a small thing, a violation that may seem not to warrant disciplinary action, may actually ruin the efficiency of the entire firehouse, putting the people the firehouse serves at risk.

7. In this passage, the word *reprimanded* means
   a. scolded.
   b. praised.
   c. rewarded.
   d. fired.

Question type: _____

8. The best title for this passage would be
   a. "Broken Windows: Only the First Step."
   b. "The Importance of Housewatch."
   c. "How to Write an Administrative Journal."
   d. "A Guide to Window Repair."

Question type: _____

9. The passage suggests that
   a. firefighters are sloppy administrators.
   b. firefighters will blame others for mistakes.
   c. discipline starts with small infractions.
   d. discipline is important for the efficiency of the firehouse.

Question type: _____

10. According to the passage, which of the following could be the result of broken windows?

    a. The building would soon be vandalized.

    b. Firefighters would lose morale.

    c. There could be a management crisis.

    d. The efficiency of the firehouse could be destroyed.

Question type: _____

ANSWERS

    7. a. *Reprimanded* means *scolded.* (Vocabulary)

    8. a. The passage is about the "broken window" theory, showing that a minor violation or breach of discipline can lead to major violations. (Main idea)

    9. d. The passage applies the broken window theory to firehouse discipline, showing that even small infractions have to be dealt with to avoid worse problems later. (Inference)

    10. a. See the third sentence of the passage. (Detail)

▶ ANSWERING STRATEGIES

Answering many multiple-choice questions correctly requires either direct knowledge or recognition and recall of specific facts, or the ability to understand written information well enough to answer questions based on that written information.

A successful test taker will approach multiple-choice questions with several good strategies. They include:

1. Unless instructed not to write on the test paper, always circle or **underline the key words in the stem** that direct your search for the answer. In the earlier examples, *president* was the key word in question 2, and *the same or almost the same* were the key words in question 4.

2. **Eliminate immediately all clearly incorrect distractors.** This will usually mean that you have to choose between two similar choices.

3. **Beware of examiners' tricks to confuse you:** look-alike options, easily confused options, silly options. Watch for tricky wordings such as "All of the following are true *except . . .*"

> **Use Your Test Booklet!**
> Unless you are forbidden to write in your test booklet, make good use of the margins and white space to note questions, make diagrams, or do calculations. Underline, circle, and draw boxes around key words for phrases in the stem.

4. **Read stems carefully** to be sure you understand *exactly* what is being asked. You will find distractors that are accurate and may sound right but do not apply to that stem. This is particularly true of options that say "All of the above" or "none of the above."

5. **Be familiar with the kinds of questions that are asked on multiple-choice tests.** This way you can quickly identify what you are looking for in a question.

6. **Beware of the absolute!** Read carefully any stem that includes words like *always*, *never*, *none*, or *all*. An answer may sound perfectly correct, and the general principal may be correct. However, it may not be true in all circumstances. For example, think about the statement "All roses are red." ALL roses?

7. **Do the easiest questions first.** Many tests are arranged so that the questions move from easy to more difficult. Don't lose out on easier points by skipping over those early questions and risk running out of time.

8. When answering questions with fairly lengthy stems, **read the options before you read the stem.** Then, when you read the question, you will already know what information you are seeking.

▶ MORE MULTIPLE-CHOICE QUESTIONS

So far, you've seen how multiple-choice questions can be designed to trigger you recall and recognition of learned material. But multiple-choice questions can be used to test other things as well.

Multiple-choice questions can test math skills because they can require specific mastery of math operations, and they can require you to choose answers that appear correct in comparison to other choices. Multiple-choice questions can also determine how well you can read graphs, maps, charts, and diagrams and pull information from them.

MULTIPLE-CHOICE MATH QUESTIONS

Math questions appear on tests for a couple of reasons. In the GED or SAT, examiners may be looking for levels of competence or achievement in math.

Some questions are mostly numerical in format:

1. What is the reciprocal of $3\frac{7}{8}$?

    a. $\frac{31}{28}$

    b. $\frac{8}{31}$

    c. $\frac{8}{21}$

    d. $\frac{31}{8}$

Some questions are introduced by stems in which the needed numerical information is embedded:

2. A city worker is paid time-and-a-half an hour in overtime pay. He earns $20 per hour. If he works four hours more than his contracted work week, how much does he make in overtime pay?

   a. $80

   b. $120

   c. $400

   d. $60

Answers

1. b. $3\frac{7}{8} = \frac{31}{8}$, whose reciprocal is $\frac{8}{31}$.

2. b. The worker makes $20 \times 1\frac{1}{2} = \$30$ per hour in overtime. Now multiply the hourly overtime wage by the number of overtime hours: $30 \times 4 = 120$.

STRATEGIES FOR ANSWERING MATH QUESTIONS

Even though you're dealing with numbers and not words in math questions, the way you analyze the questions and consider the possible answers is very similar to the types of word questions you've learned about in this chapter so far.

- Read the stem carefully. Underline or circle the most important information in the stem.
- Read all the options carefully. Don't be confused by look-alike numbers.
- Work the problem. If you see an answer that matches, you can move right on. Do all calculations on paper, not in your head.
- Skip unfamiliar questions on the first pass through the test. Put a dot in the margin of the test so you can locate the question quickly if you are in a hurry.
- Be careful when you write your calculations. The number 1 can look like 7, 3 like 8, and 6 like 0 when you are in a hurry. You risk picking up a wrong answer or wasting time recalculating an answer to find something that fits from your choice of answers.
- Translate numbers from math into English. (*Reciprocal* in question 1 means the *inverse of the fractional number.*)
- Translate words from English into math. (*Time-and-a-half* in question 2 means $1\frac{1}{2}$ or $\frac{3}{2}$.)

QUESTIONS ABOUT GRAPHIC MATERIAL

Graphic material consists of maps, charts, graphs, illustrations, or diagrams that summarize a sizable amount of information in a compact, visual format. Like some math applications, questions based on graphic material are used to test the skill of the test taker in pulling information from nonverbal sources.

Following are two kinds of graphic representations.

Causes of Household Fires, in percentages

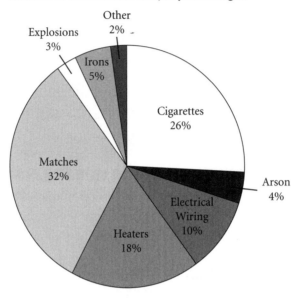

3. What is the percentage of smoking-related fires?
   a. 26%
   b. 32%
   c. 58%
   d. 26% to 58%

4. Based on the information provided in the chart, which of the following reasons applies to the majority of these fires?
   a. malicious intent to harm
   b. violation of fire safety codes
   c. carelessness
   d. faulty products

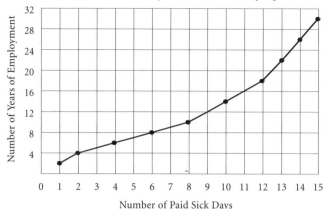

Number of Sick Days Per Year of Employment

Number of Years of Employment (vertical axis)

Number of Paid Sick Days (horizontal axis)

5. At which point does the rate of increase of sick days change?

    a. four years of employment

    b. ten years of employment

    c. eight years of employment

    d. 12 years of employment

Answers

  3. d. Both cigarettes (26%) and matches (32%) are smoking related, but not all match fires are necessarily smoking related. So, the best answer allows for a range between 26 and 58%.

  4. c. Fires from cigarettes, heaters, irons, and matches—81% in all—are most likely the result of carelessness.

  5. b. At ten years of employment, the rate of increase goes up from two days every two years to four days every two years.

STRATEGIES FOR ANSWERING GRAPHIC QUESTIONS

- Don't rush to choose your answer; spend a few minutes analyzing each graphic first.
- Translate the components of the graphic—axes on a line graph, slices of a pie chart, for example—into their verbal counterpart (for example, from the graphics here, causes of household fires or numbers of sick days per year of employment).
- Read all options carefully.
- Think about how the information shown in the graphic makes sense in real-life terms. Should paid sick leave be tied to number of years employed? What *would* be the major causes of household fires?

- Remember that you don't have to have specific information before you come to the test. Everything you need is given to you in the graphic.

On the following page, write some of the question types discussed in this chapter. If you can write one, you can answer one!

IN SHORT

Most standardized tests use the multiple-choice format for many questions. The three main elements of multiple-choice questions are stems, options, and distractors. Many multiple-choice questions measure reading comprehension and math. Strategies for answering multiple-choice questions include circling the key words or numbers in the stem of the questions, immediately eliminating all clearly incorrect distractors, and becoming familiar with the different kinds of questions that are asked.

TRY OUT YOUR READING COMPREHENSION QUESTION SKILLS

Read the following passage. Then write one of each of the four types of multiple-choice questions, based on the content of the passage.

Detectives who routinely investigate violent crimes can't help but become somewhat jaded. Paradoxically, the victims and witnesses with whom they closely work are often in a highly vulnerable and emotional state. The emotional fallout from a robbery, for example, can be complex and long-lasting. Detectives must be trained to handle people in emotional distress and must be sensitive to the fact that for the victim the crime is not routine. At the same time, detectives must recognize the limits of their role and resist the temptation to act as therapists or social workers instead of referring victims to the proper agencies.

1. A main idea question

_____

   a.

   b.

   c.

   d.

2. A detail question

_____

   a.

   b.

   c.

   d.

3. A vocabulary question

_____

   a.

   b.

   c.

   d.

4. An inference question

_____

_____

a.

b.

c.

d.

TRY OUT YOUR READING COMPREHENSION QUESTION SKILLS

(Sample answers)

1. A main idea question

   What is the main idea of the passage?
   a. Detectives who investigate violent crime must never become emotionally hardened by the experience.
   b. Victims of violent crime should be referred to therapists and social workers.
   c. Detectives should be sensitive to the emotional state of victims of violent crime.
   d. Detectives should be particularly careful in dealing with victims of sexual assault.

2. A detail question

   Which of the following would be an appropriate response by a detective to a victim in emotional distress?
   a. immediate assistance
   b. a sympathetic ear
   c. arrest of the perpetrator
   d. referral to social service agencies

3. A vocabulary question

   In this passage, the word *jaded* means
   a. nervous.
   b. lazy.
   c. insensitive.
   d. hostile.

4. An inference question

   The passage suggests that police detectives
   a. are often arrogant in dealing with victims.
   b. should be sympathetic to victims.
   c. have responsibilities beyond the arrest of criminals.
   d. are underpaid.

TRY OUT YOUR MATH QUESTION SKILLS

Answer the following sample multiple-choice questions in math and graphics.

1. A sanitation worker earns a salary of $28,000 per year. This year he will earn a 3% raise. What is his new salary?
   a. $840
   b. $28,540
   c. $37,300
   d. $28,840

2. The speed limit on Maple Drive is 30 miles per hour. The speed limit on the expressway is $1\frac{1}{2}$ times faster than the Maple Drive limit. What is the speed limit on the expressway?
   a. 65 mph
   b. 15 mph
   c. 45 mph
   d. 20 mph

Compact Discs Sold

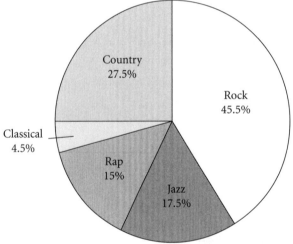

3. Which types of music represent exactly half of the compact disks sold?
   a. rock and jazz
   b. classical and rock
   c. rap, classical, and country
   d. jazz, country, and rap

ANSWERS

1. d. Multiply the salary by 3%, or .03: $28,000 \times .03 = 840$. Now add this increase to the original salary to get $28,840.

2. c. Multiply 30 by $1\frac{1}{2}$, or $\frac{3}{2}$, to get 45 miles per hour.

3. b. Rock is 45.5% and classical 4.5%.

Other Types of Questions on the Classroom Test

While multiple-choice questions are the ones that usually come to mind when you think about tests, classroom exams are usually made up of a variety of short-answer questions. Different formats test different types of information and various ways of demonstrating skills and knowledge.

▶ WHAT QUESTIONS CAN YOU EXPECT?

You have seen that most test questions on standardized tests are presented in the multiple-choice format. In the classroom, however, there are a number of question formats that are commonly used along with or instead of multiple-choice questions to allow an examiner to determine how much you are learning in a course.

RECOGNITION QUESTIONS

There are two types of recognition questions:

- True/false—tell whether the statements represent accurate or inaccurate information
- Matching two lists—match the words or terms in one column with those that most apply in the other.

RECALL QUESTIONS

There are three kinds of recall questions:

- Completions—supply words needed to complete the idea of the statement or sentence
- Identifications—define words, terms, or names from memory
- Essays—develop extended answers, usually one or more paragraphs, from your own knowledge of the topic (essay writing is covered in Chapters 11–13)

▶ WHY SO MANY KINDS OF QUESTIONS?

Unlike writers of standardized exams, an individual class teacher can construct tests to suit individual goals, both philosophical and practical.

PHILOSOPHICAL PURPOSES

Teachers want to make sure that tests do a good job of testing many things.

- A variety of questions in a variety of formats gives students with different learning strengths several opportunities to demonstrate their abilities and knowledge. Some people recall facts easily and do well on short-answer tests. Others are better at expressing themselves in essay writing.
- Exams often need to test a wide range of material, and one kind of question format can't cover it all.
- The instructor wants to test both recognition of key concepts in the material and the recall of information and must use different types of questions to test both.

PRACTICAL PURPOSES

There are also some straightforward reasons for varying question format. These include:

- Some kinds of questions are easier for the instructor to write, so they're used along with more complex questions.
- An instructor may have time constraints, which means that at least some of the questions have to be in a short-answer format because they take less time to grade.
- It's more interesting to grade a variety of questions on a large number of test papers. (And it's more interesting for you as a test taker, too.)

▶ STRATEGIES FOR ANSWERING QUESTIONS

How you approach a question depends on what type of question it is.

TRUE/FALSE QUESTIONS

True/false questions are statements that you must identify as accurate or inaccurate based on your knowledge of the subject. Answering such questions correctly is not always just a matter of knowing whether a statement is factually correct. Instructors often use true/false tests to see how carefully you read the questions. Here are some things to watch for.

Questions That Contain Absolutes or Other Qualifiers

Absolutes are statements that offer no alternatives. Words that are absolutes include *always, never, best, worst, none, all, only, everyone,* and *no one,* as in this example:

Students should *never* study immediately before sleep. True or false?

Another type of qualifier is an addition to a basic statement that gives it a different meaning, as in the example here:

Students should allow *very little* time to pass between study and sleep. True or false?

In the first example, you would immediately eliminate True because the statement is an absolute. Very few things in life are absolute, and absolute statements on tests are almost always false. In the second example, the qualifier makes the statement sound reasonable. As you read in Chapter 3, sleep should follow study with little or no interference, so the second statement is True.

Questions That Contain Negatives

Be alert for prefixes to words and words themselves that make the statement mean the opposite of the truth, as in these examples:

Students should *not* plan to sleep immediately after study.

Research generally shows that it is *un*wise to sleep immediately after study.

If you recall from Chapter 3 that going to sleep right after studying improves the chances of retention, then making this fact negative—by having the negative word in the first and the negative prefix in the second—makes both statements false.

Questions with Information Designed to Mislead

A question with misleading information in it can confuse the real issue at hand, as in this example:

Students may *watch television* between sleep and study, but should not *listen to the radio* between sleep and study.

The real issue here is whether or not it is wise to do anything between studying and sleeping. You know from Chapter 3 that it is best to go right to sleep after studying. Therefore, one should not listen to the radio *or* watch television between studying and sleeping, so this statement is false.

Some questions are written to confuse the student by adding false information to an answer that would otherwise be true. For example, "Environmentalists concerned about the impact of global warming cite the greenhouse effect and comprehensive health care as matters demanding government attention." Environmentalists may be interested in the greenhouse effect where global warming is concerned, but health care would not be the concern of that same group. In order for an answer to be true, all the parts of the answer must be true.

MATCHING COLUMNS

The main thing to remember when you are taking a matching column test is to read both columns carefully before matching *anything*. Once you have read both lists all the way through you can start to match the two pieces that belong together. Remember that the correct answers are there for you. It merely remains for you to make good choices among those that seem to match up. Here are some ways of making these good choices:

1. Start with the first item in column A. Search all the way through column B until you locate the best answer. You may see more than one as you work your way down the column, so don't be hasty in making your choice.

2. When you have made a choice from column B, draw a circle around it so that you know it's out of the running for the time being. Don't scratch it out because you may want to take another look at it later if you have doubts about your first choice. If you have scratched it out, you may not be able to see it to reconsider.

3. If you don't find a match for one term, don't waste time searching right away. Leave it blank and come back to it when you have fewer choices available to you.

4. If you find a second match and are unsure of which is the better choice, write the letters of both choices beside the term in column A and return to them later. You will probably find that one of your choices has been taken for another item.

5. Remember that most instructors add one or two extra choices to column B so that you can't work entirely by the process of elimination. Sometimes these extra items are silly and you can eliminate them easily. But sometimes they're tricky because the instructor has chosen a sound-alike or look-alike term to confuse you.

6. When you write the letter of the match in column A, remember to write your letters carefully so that the letter *I* doesn't look like the letter *L*, *G*s like *Q*s, and *M*s like *N*s.

Match the following columns for practice.

Column A	Column B
_____ **1.** annotations	**a.** last-minute, intensive study
_____ **2.** mnemonics	**b.** diagram of key ideas in text
_____ **3.** mapping	**c.** intermittent study
_____ **4.** cramming	**d.** memory losses
_____ **5.** distributed practice	**e.** margin summaries
	f. memory tricks

Note that choices **a** and **c** and choices **d** and **f** could easily be mistaken for each other. Here are the correct answers:

Column A	Column B
<u>e</u> **1.** annotations	**a.** last-minute, intensive study
<u>f</u> **2.** mnemonics	**b.** diagram of key ideas in text
<u>b</u> **3.** mapping	**c.** intermittent study
<u>a</u> **4.** cramming	**d.** memory losses
<u>c</u> **5.** distributed practice	**e.** margin summaries
	f. memory tricks

COMPLETION QUESTIONS

These questions are made up of a stem or partial statement that has to be completed to make sense. Completion questions, along with identification questions, are the hardest of the short-answer formats because they rely almost entirely on your recall of information. There are some ways of looking at these questions, though, that may be helpful:

1. Watch for clue words in the *stem* of the question.

Two ways to X-ray text for main ideas are _____ and _____.

The term *X-ray* may trigger your memory of *mapping* and *annotating*.

2. Watch for clues in the *words* in the question.

_____ comes from a medical term that means that you sort out the wounded into *three* categories of seriousness. In this book, it refers to determining which subjects you should give priority to and which you should spend the most time studying for an upcoming test or tests.

If you know that the prefix for three is *tri-*, you may more easily recall that the word you're looking for is *triage*.

3. Watch for *grammatical* clues in the question.

An _____ learner learns best by listening.

Of the three types of learners you've read about earlier in this book, only *auditory* can take the article *an.* The terms *visual* and *kinesthetic* would need to be introduced by the article *a.* (A good teacher, though, won't give you such a clue. He or she would write "a/an" instead.)

IDENTIFICATIONS

Identifications are words and terms you need to recognize and then be able to define or explain in your own words. Identifications are often names of people, procedures, places, historical locations, or events. On literature tests, you may have to identify important characters in a book or play.

This kind of question leaves you very much on your own to retrieve what you remember about the word or term and to express that information clearly. Here's some good advice for answering identification questions:

1. If you don't recall the correct spelling, spell the definition as best you can. Don't leave a space blank because you can't spell the answer. Get at least partial credit.
2. Make your definitions as brief as possible. The instructor is not looking for an essay, just a sense that you are familiar with the term.
3. If you don't remember a name, term, or fact exactly, write what you think you do know about it, like the test taker did in the following examples.

Identifications on a test about twentieth-century women authors:
Betty Friedan: wrote *The Feminine Misteke* (sp?)
The Bloomsbury set: a group of writers in London, I think in the 1920s
Ayn Rand: wrote about the importance of individualism

On page 97, try your hand at playing teacher. Write a classroom test on the content of this book so far, using several different types of question formats. A completed sample follows, although your answers will be different.

IN SHORT

Classroom tests may use true/false, matching, completion, and identification questions (in addition to multiple-choice and essay questions). Each kind of question has its own strategies, although reading the question carefully is always key.

CREATE YOUR OWN TEST

Use the following form to write a test on this book.

Mark the following statements as true or false.

1. _____

2. _____

3. _____

4. _____

5. _____

Match the definitions in Column B with the words in Column A.

Column A   **Column B**

___ 1. _____   a. _____

___ 2. _____   b. _____

___ 3. _____   c. _____

___ 4. _____   d. _____

___ 5. _____   e. _____

___ 6. _____   f. _____

___ 7. _____   g. _____

___ 8. _____   h. _____

___ 9. _____   i. _____

___ 10. _____   j. _____

                               k. _____

Complete the following sentences.

1. _____

2. _____

3. _____

4. _____

5. _____

Identify the following terms.

1. _____

2. _____

3. _____

4. _____

CREATE YOUR OWN TEST

(Completed sample)

Mark the following statements as true or false.

1. The library is a poor place to study.

2. Studying for long periods of time aids retention.

3. You should never exercise before an exam.

4. Study groups are sometimes good for reviewing information.

5. Family and friends can be helpful in preparing for a test.

Match the definitions in Column B with the words in Column A.

Column A		**Column B**	
___	**1.** auditory learner	**a.**	marginal summaries
___	**2.** visual modality	**b.**	pictorial information
___	**3.** map	**c.**	learning by seeing
___	**4.** distractors	**d.**	learns by listening
___	**5.** ACT	**e.**	a college admission test
___	**6.** SAT	**f.**	a classroom test
___	**7.** annotation	**g.**	possible answers
___	**8.** graphics	**h.**	a diagram of main ideas
___	**9.** stem	**i.**	the main idea of the question
___	**10.** options	**j.**	incorrect answers
		k.	a college admission test

Complete the following sentences.

1. It is convenient to write study notes on _____.

2. Sentences that ask you to supply words are called _____.

3. Tests that ask you to identify terms are called _____.

4. Words or phrases that offer no alternatives are called _____.

5. Reading comprehension questions that call for conclusions are _____ questions.

Identify the following terms.

1. mnemonics

2. triage

3. kinesthetic learning

4. cramming

IF YOU DON'T KNOW AN ANSWER TO A TEST QUESTION, DON'T ELIMINATE YOUR CHANCES BY LEAVING IT BLANK. MAKE AN EDUCATED GUESS. IN THIS CHAPTER, YOU'LL LEARN HOW TO DO JUST THAT ON MANY KINDS OF TEST QUESTIONS.

Should You Guess? Often, Yes!

You will notice that in all of the test-taking strategies noted in the last few chapters, you have read nothing about one of the most obvious approaches to test taking when the answer is not immediately clear: guessing. Most of you have taken a shot at guessing on a test, and it is likely that in some cases your guesses were correct and probably were more informed choices than you thought.

You may feel a little guilty about guessing, though. It's a little like saying, "I didn't read that chapter; I just skimmed it." If you got the meaning from the reading, you were reading, regardless of your reading technique. If you get the right answer, you got it right, whether you were guessing or not.

This is not to say, though, that you should guess wildly and without thinking at all. No. You should *choose* to guess and do it in a systematic, purposeful way.

▶ WHEN TO GUESS

You should guess when:

- There is no penalty for doing so.
- You are absolutely sure you know *nothing* about the question.
- You are unsure about a choice between two plausible answers.

However, some tests, including the SAT, deduct a quarter of a point for each incorrect answer. You can still guess on these questions, but you should be selective and make educated guesses.

▶ TAKE EDUCATED GUESSES

GUESSING ON MULTIPLE-CHOICE TESTS

As you know, multiple-choice questions usually have four or five options, only one of which is right. Theoretically, each answer gives you a 20 to 25 percent chance of being correct. If you raise the odds by eliminating one or more of those distractors right away, you are in an even better position to make a good guess. The problem is, what do you do when you have two answers that sound equally correct?

Use the True/False Test

Try submitting the stem and each of the two options you are using to a true/false test.

1. The primary responsibility of the office manager is to
   a. get the CEO's coffee promptly.
   b. oversee the general operation of the office.
   c. hire and fire other office staff.
   d. plan the office Christmas party.

After you eliminate choices **a** and **d** because they are clearly not primary responsibilities, you can look at both of the others in a true/false context.

The *primary* responsibility of the office manager is to oversee the general operation of the office. True or false?

The *primary* responsibility of the office manager is to hire and fire other staff. True or false?

Between these two, it seems clear that the truer of the statements is that the manager oversees general operations. Although she may indeed participate in hiring decisions, it is unlikely that it is her primary responsibility. Notice that the key word in the stem is *primary*.

This strategy is particularly helpful when you are given options such as *all of the above, none of the above*, or *only 2 and 4 above*.

Go for the Middle

When you are guessing on multiple-choice questions that have numerical options, look for midrange numbers among your options.

2. In the last ten years, the number of reported incidences of domestic violence has increased by
   a. 22%.
   b. 10%.
   c. 75%.
   d. 5%.

Without any other information, you may want to choose choice **a** or **b** simply because they are in the middle of the range provided by all four answers.

In classroom tests, it often seems that the correct answer among multiple-choice options is the longest or the one in the middle. (This seems to be less true in standardized tests.)

3. Research indicates that people learn most effectively when they study in
   a. a cram session.
   b. two short sessions.
   c. several short sessions over a period of time.
   d. one long session.
   e. groups.

If you've been reading this book carefully, you don't have to guess on this question. But if you didn't have a clue, and if this were a classroom test, you might go for choice **c** just because it's longest.

Try Your Best-Guess Strategies First

Choose the middle or the longest option only when you have absolutely no clue as to the correct answer and have exhausted more informed approaches. Also, be aware that many test makers know that people have a tendency to guess this way and guard against it by not putting the correct option in the middle or making it the longest one.

GUESSING ON TRUE/FALSE QUESTIONS

On classroom tests, there are more likely to be more true answers than false ones because false answers are harder for the instructor to write. Therefore, if you have to take a guess, choosing True is probably the better bet.

Be careful of tricky wording in true/false questions.

Negatives

Negatives in a statement turn it into its opposite meaning.

> **4.** Dispute over states' rights was not a major cause of the U.S. Civil War. True or false?

To test the truth of this kind of question, simply take out the negative word and see if the question is true. Negatives in a statement can be confusing because people are not accustomed to reading something when it's in negative terms.

Absolutes

Absolutes qualify a statement to an extreme. You'll recall from Chapter 8 that you should be wary of words like *all, always, solely, never, none, best,* and *worst.* On true/false tests, however, these words can help you because they usually signal that a statement is false.

> **5.** Smoking tobacco has been responsible for all forms of respiratory disease. True or false?

On the basis of the absolute, here the word *all,* you would choose False.

Word Structure

Use anything you know about vocabulary and structure to trigger recognition or recall of information.

> **6.** Bicameral government has two houses in the legislature. True or false?

If you remember that the prefix *bi-* means two, then you'd make an educated guess that this statement is true.

GUESSING ON MATCHING COLUMNS

Success at guessing on matching columns depends on how many guesses you have to make. If you are guessing between two choices, the odds are the same as those on true/false—50 percent. If you are guessing at more than two, your odds are lower on each answer. So, you should begin by reading all of the options. Then, begin by matching those you are certain of, thereby reducing the number of difficult matches you have left to guess.

GUESSING ON COMPLETION QUESTIONS

It's hard to guess on questions that require retrieval of information, but some instructors will give partial credit for inexact answers that nevertheless answer the spirit of the question.

7. A _____ economic policy is one in which the government allows the private sector to dominate.

If you couldn't remember *laissez faire*, but did remember what it meant, you could have written *hands off* and may have received partial credit.

Sometimes, a guesser is aided by a careless test maker who will give away clues such as the *a/an* advantage. In such a case, if there is the word *an* before the blank, then you can assume that the correct answer starts with a vowel.

8. The group represented a _____ religious faith.

If the test taker were torn between two words, for example, *evangelical* and *Pentecostal*, the *a* would give it away. *Pentecostal* is correct because it is introduced by *a*. Wise test makers, however, cover themselves in these matters by putting *a/an* before such blanks.

On the next page, see how well you can figure out the answers to questions based on guessing strategies alone.

IN SHORT

If you don't know the answer to a question, make an educated guess. Turn multiple-choice questions into true/false questions to test each possible answer. Watch out for the use of negatives in true/false statements and be wary of absolutes, such as *none, never, all, always,* and *best*. Even if you don't remember the complete answer for a short-answer question, write down what you do know because you may receive partial credit.

TEST YOUR GUESS-ABILITY

Without any information to guide you on these questions, see what educated guesses you can make. Then, take a look at the answer sheet to see how well you did.

Multiple-choice questions

1. When not responding directly to a fire, a firefighter's main responsibility is
   a. maintaining the firefighting apparatus.
   b. upholding the image of the department in the community.
   c. delegating responsibilities in the firehouse.
   d. keeping in good physical condition.

2. Dr. Martin Luther King led the March on Washington in
   a. 1960.
   b. 1963.
   c. 1972.
   d. 1985.

3. A reader's ability to comprehend what he or she is reading depends upon
   a. intelligence.
   b. reading speed.
   c. prior knowledge or familiarity with the content.
   d. phonics.
   e. whole language.

True/false questions

_____ 1. Preservation of the union was not a primary consideration in the American Civil War.
_____ 2. All greenhouse gases are harmful to humans.
_____ 3. Recycling does not materially affect environmental quality.
_____ 4. Geology is the study of the earth and its properties.
_____ 5. Gandhi's call for nonviolent resistance failed to unite his country against colonial rule.

Completions

1. The botanical term for plant reproduction is _____.
2. A plant that goes to seed and dies at the end of the growing season is called an _____.

TEST YOUR GUESS-ABILITY

(Answer sheet)

Multiple-choice questions

1. When not responding directly to a fire, a firefighter's main responsibility is
   - **a.** maintaining the firefighting apparatus.
   - **b.** upholding the image of the department in the community.
   - **c.** delegating responsibilities in the firehouse.
   - **d.** keeping in good physical condition.

2. Dr. Martin Luther King led the March on Washington in
   - **a.** 1960.
   - **b.** 1963.
   - **c.** 1972.
   - **d.** 1985.

3. A reader's ability to comprehend what he or she is reading depends upon
   - **a.** intelligence.
   - **b.** reading speed.
   - **c.** prior knowledge or familiarity with the content.
   - **d.** phonics.
   - **e.** whole language.

True/false questions

- _F_ **1.** Preservation of the union was not a primary consideration in the American Civil War.
- _F_ **2.** All greenhouse gases are harmful to humans.
- _F_ **3.** Recycling does not materially affect environmental quality.
- _T_ **4.** Geology is the study of the earth and its properties.
- _F_ **5.** Gandhi's call for nonviolent resistance failed to unite his country against colonial rule.

Completions

1. The botanical term for plant reproduction is propagate.
2. A plant that goes to seed and dies at the end of the growing season is called an annual.

Managing Your Time during a Short-Answer Test

I n Chapters 7–9, you met the kinds of multiple-choice and other questions you might encounter on tests, and learned how you can make educated guesses on questions of which you are unsure.

Now that you know how to approach short-answer questions and even take educated guesses, let's look at how to handle those questions under testing conditions. It goes without saying that it's very important for you to plan and pace your approach to tests carefully. There are few things more disappointing than losing control of a test after long and sometimes painful preparation!

▶ BEFORE YOU START

PREVIEW THE TEST

There should be no surprises when you get to any section of the test. It's like taking a trip through the woods: It's helpful to know where you are going and what you will encounter along the way.

There are two reasons why you should preview a test very carefully before you start working:

- You want to find out where the more difficult parts are on the test, so you can prepare to spend more time on those sections.
- You want to be familiar with the content of the whole test so that you have a good overall picture of what topics are stressed and know the formats for all of the sections of the test. Then, as you go back and work through the test, you're revisiting familiar ground.

ARE SECTIONS TIMED?

See if each section of the test has been assigned a time frame.

Vocabulary:	20 minutes
Reading Comprehension:	40 minutes
Math Computation:	30 minutes
Verbal Expression:	30 minutes

If you are allowed to write in the test booklet, circle those times so you are well aware of how long you have for each section.

HOW LONG IS THE TEST?

Count or take note of the number of pages in the test. The reason for this will be clear later.

READ OR LISTEN TO DIRECTIONS CAREFULLY

If allowed, always underline or circle key words in the instructions that cue you to what the question requires. Follow the directions to the letter. This will be covered in more detail later.

▶ GETTING STARTED

ASSIGN TIMES TO SECTIONS

If there is no time frame already allowed for each section of the test, quickly figure out how much time you think you will need to allow for each section. Base your assessment on your best guess of what sections will be easiest for you. For example, if you feel more comfortable in math, allow for less time there than for the sections that will be tougher for you, like reading. If you're allowed to write in the test booklet, quickly jot down a time allowance for each section in the margin at the start of each section.

For example, a standardized test may include the following in a one-hour test. Based merely on your own comfort level, how much time would you allot to each of the following sections for that hour?

Vocabulary	8 questions	____ minutes
Comprehension	3 paragraphs with 10 questions	____ minutes
Math	22 questions	____ minutes
Punctuation	10 questions	____ minutes
Grammar	10 questions	____ minutes
Spelling	10 questions	____ minutes

MATCH TIME TO TEST POINTS

Note how much each section of a test counts in terms of total test points. It is foolish to waste time fretting over short-answer questions that count less than an essay that's worth much more. If you've sketched out in your mind how much time you want to spend on each section, you will know when you're beginning to waste time. Plan to spend longer on the sections that count more. If you haven't finished one section and it is time to go on to another that carries more points, do so.

DON'T LINGER TOO LONG ON ANY ONE QUESTION

Answer the questions in a section or on the whole test that you know the answers to for certain right away. If you are unsure about a question, put a dot in the margin next to that question so you can find it easily when you want to come back to it later. Don't linger too long over questions you can't answer right away. You may find that other questions on the test will steer you to the best choices for questions that at first seem difficult to you.

NOTE SPECIAL DIRECTIONS

Take special note of directions involving choice or selection. For example, if in the directions for a section of 15 examples, it says, "Write definitions for ten of the following," don't write definitions for all 15! You won't get any bonus points for doing all 15, nor will the instructor search around the test paper for your *best* ten. You'll only waste precious time.

▶ HOW TO AVOID PANIC

There are times when you may feel absolutely panicked in the middle of a test. If you are feeling shaky because you see too many unfamiliar questions on the test, are running out of time, or have just run out of energy for a while, here are some techniques for keeping yourself from coming unglued:

1. Stop writing for a minute or two and relax.
2. Sit back in your chair. Let your arms and head drop down and breathe slowly and deeply for a few seconds.
3. Try to empty your mind of all its worries. Visualize the end of the test.
4. Stretch your arms, hands, neck, and shoulders.
5. Take off your sweater. Put on your sweater.
6. Blow your nose, or pop a mint in your mouth.
7. Return to the test with a get-tough attitude.

Sometimes, you have to make a triage decision about the test. For instance, decide where on the test you can earn the most points in the time you have left. Concentrate on doing the very best you can in those areas. You'll feel better when you have regained control over yourself and over the test.

▶ WHEN YOU HAVE TIME LEFT

If you've followed the suggestions in these chapters and conscientiously maintained control over the timing, you may find that you have time left over after you have finished the test. Do not throw down your pen and sigh with relief that the test is over—at least not yet! Remember, this is not a race. You don't win by being first over the finish line. Resist the temptation to leave right away.

Here are some suggestions for making the best possible use of any time left over.

DON'T LEAVE ANYTHING OUT
Make sure you don't have any unfinished business:

- Count the pages of the test booklet again. Double-check that you didn't skip a page because two pages stuck together or you accidentally turned two pages at the same time. Now is the time to do any work you missed this way. Imagine losing credit for a whole section on the test because you didn't see it and didn't do it! It happens.
- Go back and look for any questions you were uncertain about. This is why it's wise to put a dot in the margin next to tough questions. When you don't have much time at the end of a test, you want to make it as easy as possible to find those questions you were unsure about earlier.

- Look at the problem questions with a fresh pair of eyes. They may not seem as difficult or confusing as they did the first time you saw them. They may be clearer in light of other questions you've now answered.
- If you have unanswered questions left, decide whether it's best to leave them blank or take an educated guess in hopes of getting some credit. Remember the tips for smart guessing in Chapter 9.

DOUBLE-CHECK YOUR ANSWERS

After you've made sure you've answered (or decided not to answer) all the questions, check for accuracy and completeness in your answers.

- Make sure each answer you've chosen is entered in the correct spot on the answer sheet and is legibly written. Second only to the frustration at having missed whole sections accidentally is the irritation of having put correct answers in the wrong places on the answer sheet.
- Make sure your numbers and letters are clear and carefully written. You don't want to have your 4 look like a 9, or an *M* be read as an *N*.
- If you change an answer, make sure you change it completely. Write the new answer down before you erase the old answer.
- If you change an answer, be doubly sure of its accuracy now. Generally speaking, your first choices are the best choices on short-answer questions. If you change your mind, it should be for some specific reason, not just a gut feeling or intuition. Check essays for grammar and punctuation. Make sure there's nothing you want to add to the text (see Chapter 13).

Give yourself some practice in planning and pacing a test by using the following page to make a time schedule for one of the sample tests in Chapters 14–15. A completed sample follows.

IN SHORT

You can manage your time during short-answer tests by previewing the test before you begin. Look to see if the sections have time limits and write them down. Estimate how long it will take you to complete each section and note any special directions about how points are calculated. If you have extra time left at the end of the test, review your work and complete any questions you left blank during your first time through the test.

TIME SCHEDULE FOR _____

TEST IN CHAPTER _____

Preview the tests in Chapter 14–15 and choose one. Write a time schedule for that test.

Section	Minutes
_____	_____
_____	_____
_____	_____
_____	_____
_____	_____
_____	_____
_____	_____

TIME SCHEDULE FOR STANDARDIZED
TEST IN CHAPTER 14

(Completed sample)

Section	Minutes
Vocabulary	10
Spelling	5
Grammar/Punctuation	5
Language Expression	10
Math	10
Reading Comprehension	20

IN THIS CHAPTER, YOU'LL LEARN HOW TO GET READY TO TAKE AN ESSAY OR EXTENDED-ANSWER TEST, WITH STRATEGIES FOR PREDICTING QUESTION TOPICS IN ADVANCE.

Preparing for Essay Questions

Essay and extended-answer questions require not only that you remember or recall facts, but also that you organize and present these facts in a written summary. Unlike short-answer questions, these longer answers are usually considered to be subjective because they ask you to give your own interpretation to the information.

Essays are usually at least one paragraph in length and organized into a structure that includes an introduction, development of one or more ideas, and a conclusion. An extended-answer question is similar to a short-answer completion question, except that it requires more than just a word or phrase. It may ask for one or more complete sentences, a list, definitions, or steps in a process.

▶ WHY ARE ESSAYS SO POPULAR ON EXAMS?

Essay and extended-answer questions are used on exams because they allow an instructor to test for—and a student to demonstrate—different kinds of skills and knowledge than those assessed on a multiple-choice or short-answer test.

ADVANTAGES

Essay and extended-answer questions allow:

- The instructor to ask for proof of a wider knowledge of the subject than can be asked for in a short-answer question
- The student to demonstrate some breadth of knowledge beyond the range of the question itself
- An opportunity for those students whose strengths are in writing or communications to show their talents
- The instructor to gauge the writing skills of the student as well as the student's knowledge of the subject

DISADVANTAGES

The disadvantages of essay and extended-answer questions are:

- They are time-consuming to take.
- They are time-consuming to grade.
- They are graded partly on the instructor's judgment of your writing skill rather than strictly on the knowledge you show in answering the actual question.
- They may penalize students whose language and writing skills are less well developed.

▶ WHAT DO YOU STUDY?

If you know that a large percentage of a test is going to be comprised of essay and extended-answer questions, you have to prepare for the test in specific ways.

CLASS NOTES

Do a thorough review of all your class notes. Start with these notes because most instructors have specific matters and viewpoints that they repeat fairly often through the semester. List specific ideas that were raised in lectures, but are not in the text.

Borrow and photocopy a set of notes from a classmate. Compare them with your own notes. Add anything that you may have missed in your own notes. You may want to write notes from other sources in a contrasting ink so that you remember where that information came from.

HANDOUTS

Next, do a thorough review of all handout materials—articles copied from newspapers, periodicals, or journals, for example—and make notes in the margins of any themes or ideas that echo those of the class notes.

TEXTBOOKS

Read the highlighted text and margin notes you made in your textbooks. List separately any ideas that reinforce or contrast the ideas in the class notes and handouts. Read the titles, subtitles, advance organizers (margin notes or headings that alert you to what is in the text), chapter summaries, and introductions.

Look for sections at the end of chapters that say things like *Questions to Think About*. More than one instructor has drawn test questions directly from a book's lists of questions.

▶ How to Prepare

ANALYZE YOUR PREVIOUS TEST EXPERIENCES

Look at other essay tests you have taken and been graded on. Recall the kinds of errors you may have made on those tests. And make note of instructors' comments about your essays, such as:

- doesn't answer the question
- too vague
- be careful of punctuation

FIND OUT ABOUT PAST TESTS

Get as much information as you can about previous tests by this instructor in this course.

- Ask the instructor what areas will be covered by the essay questions. Listen carefully to the answers you get.
- Ask students who have taken the course before to tell you about the instructor's tests. Listen to the *buzz* about the tests in this course. Most instructors have a reputation for being interested in specific things. Word gets around.

Where's the Emphasis?

Some instructors organize a course around their own lectures and use the textbook and handouts only as supplementary materials. Others use the book as the main source of the course and supplement it with lectures and handouts. Decide whether your course is book-centered or instructor-centered so you have some idea about what the instructor is likely to emphasize on the test.

- Do not fall for offers of previous tests that will tell you what questions will be on the test. Most instructors don't give the same test every year. It does help to know what *kind* of questions that instructor may favor, though.
- Find out whether the instructor or someone else grades the exams. You may have more leeway with an instructor who already knows your work from the class, and you could pitch your essays to those areas you know the instructor emphasized in class. If a teaching assistant grades the papers, you may have to be more specific in the language that you use and the points you raise that may have come from class discussions or personal conversations with the instructor.

BRAINSTORM WITH YOUR CLASSMATES

Group study is good for essay test preparation because groups lend themselves more to the give and take of discussion than to facts learned for short-answer recall. You can benefit from the interpretations of other minds.

Talk through concepts, philosophies, themes in literature, or other possible essay topics with your study group. Share the work of making up sample essays for an exam. Have each person in the study group contribute one possible essay question based on your conversations in the group. Then, have everyone in the group write answers for these practice essays. Compare your answers.

▶ STUDY STRATEGIES

Play instructor. Once you have assembled all the information that seems to be important for essay questions on your test, make up imaginary questions on the main ideas you have noticed in the course. Think what questions you would ask if you were the instructor.

BE FAMILIAR WITH TERMS USED IN ESSAY QUESTIONS

One way to anticipate essay questions is to know the kinds of things you may be asked to write about. The following table shows a list of the most common key words used in essay questions.

Key Words	Meaning	Example
Trace	Describe the process or development of an idea, practice, or social/political phenomenon.	Trace the development of entitlement programs in the United States since the New Deal.

Key Words	Meaning	Example
Describe	Make a detailed, sequential picture of a series of events.	Describe the main events leading to the outbreak of the U.S. Civil War in 1861.
Discuss	Analyze in considerable detail all aspects related to an event, a social or political trend, an idea, or a point of view.	Discuss the color symbolism in the novel *The Great Gatsby*.
Evaluate	Make a judgment about specific facts or circumstances. (Sometimes the word you see in questions like this is *criticize*.)	Evaluate the effort to reinstate prayer in the public schools.
Explain	Clarify and give reasons for the ideas in the material.	Explain the need for regulations in the securities industry.
Defend	Give one side of an argument and offer reasons for your opinion.	Defend the practice of diplomatic immunity.
Summarize	Condense a large amount of information into a shorter format.	Summarize the arguments supporting an increase in taxes.

There are other terms that are used for extended-answer tests. This second table shows some of the less common terms.

Key Words	Meaning	Example
Enumerate	Present information in a sequential manner.	Enumerate the stages of bereavement.
List	Make an itemized series of names or terms.	List three major civil rights initiatives in the 1960s.
Give examples	Note instances illustrating the main idea.	Give four examples of twentieth-century artistic movements.
Identify	Define or characterize names, terms, places, or events.	Identify the three branches of the federal government.

MAKE CHARTS

You may make charts similar to the study notes described in Chapter 3. They consist of the question on one half of the page and the answer on the other. The questions can be phrased in several ways that are typical of essay exams.

Here's an example of a chart for an essay question on global warming:

Global Warming

Causes	Destruction of rain forests
	Ozone depletion
Effects	Melting of the ice caps
	Changes in climate patterns
	Disruption of food production
Solutions	Decrease dependence on fossil fuels
	Ban the use of CFCs
	Preserve the rain forest

Other charts could show:

- **Comparisons/contrasts.** Compare the Red Scares of the 1920s with the Communist witchhunts of the 1950s.
- **Pros and cons.** (or benefits/risks or advantages/disadvantages). Describe the arguments for and against a balanced budget amendment in Congress.
- **Theories/theorists, writers/works.** Evaluate the contributions of feminist writers in the Women's Liberation movement of the 1970s.

The benefit of the chart format is that you can fold the paper lengthwise and quiz yourself with the questions on one side, and then check your answers on the other.

MAKE FLASH CARDS

Flash cards can be a great help when you're learning factual information for short-answer tests—and they can be just as helpful when studying for essays. In fact, you may be able to use some of your factual cards to provide the details you need for a good essay answer.

Flash cards for preparing for essays can be organized as follows:

- Sort flash cards into piles that pertain to specific topics.
- On the face of a clean card, write a sample essay question for each pile of cards.

- Put the question card and all the cards that pertain to that question together. Review the cards often over a period of time before the test. Your constant review of the subject matter will help you respond to any question you may be asked on that topic.
- Make note cards that contain the main facts you want to include on specific essays. This will reduce a large number of facts to a small number of notes that you can carry with you to review when you have any spare time throughout the day.

MAKE OUTLINES

Imagine some essay questions you may be asked on your test. Then write outlines of your essay answers. Outlining streamlines the information you want to remember to include in an essay. Here is an example:

Define global warming. Describe the proposed risks of global warming. Suggest possible solutions to the problem of global warming.

I. What is global warming?
II. Risks of global warming
    A. Melting ice caps
    B. Changes in climate patterns
    C. Disrupted food production
III. Solutions to global warming
    A. Preserve the rain forests
    B. Reduce dependence on fossil fuels
    C. Reduce uses of CFCs

MAP THE MAIN IDEAS

If you are a highly visual learner, you may want to prepare your practice essays by making a diagram or map of the main points you need to remember. Like the X-ray strategy described in Chapter 3, mapping shows just the skeleton of the essay, but it's easy to retrieve and then flesh out when you're actually taking the test.

On the following page, make study plans to prepare for essay questions you think may be included on a test based on this book.

IN SHORT

Essays and extended-answer questions are popular on classroom exams because they allow the instructor to test the student's breadth of knowledge and writing skills at the same time. You can prepare for these types of questions by studying your class notes, handouts, and textbooks. Get together with other students to form a study group and make flash cards to carry with you for daily review.

Practice preparing for an essay test by using the study strategies explained in this chapter. Then, compare your study strategies with those on the completed sample.

Make a comparison chart on the benefits and drawbacks of essay questions on tests.

Outline the principal kinds of multiple-choice questions included in this book.

Map the two main question formats with examples of each.

Make flash cards for the steps needed to avoid panic on a test.

(Completed sample)

Make a comparison chart on the benefits and drawbacks of essay questions on tests.

Benefits	Drawbacks
wider knowledge	time-consuming to take
show verbal strength	time-consuming to grade
test writing skills	use judgment
show more knowledge	penalize poor skills

Outline the principal kinds of multiple-choice questions included in this book.

I. Recognition
   A. Facts
   B. Reading comprehension
II. Recall
   A. Math and graphic aids
   B. Common sense and reasoning

Map the two main question formats with examples of each.

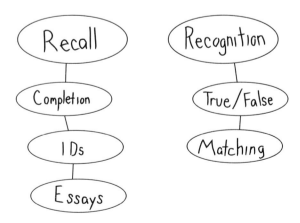

Make flash cards for the steps needed to avoid panic on a test.

Stop writing:
  Breathe deeply
  Visualize success

Be physical:
  Stretch
  Take off/put on sweater
  Eat a mint or chew gum
  Get tough!

Taking an Essay Test

s writing essay answers on tests different from writing essays for an English class? Yes and no. There are some similarities. For instance, you need to be clear and accurate as well as grammatically correct, and you must communicate what you know to someone else. The difference in writing essays for exams is that you must write within a time limit, and you have to organize your thoughts without the benefit of a textbook or notes.

▶ How to Get Started

READ ALL THE QUESTIONS FIRST

It is particularly important to read all the questions first because sometimes questions are related to each other. You don't want to waste all your good points on one question when you may be able to use them on two or more questions.

You also want to be alerted to the subjects of the test so that you can allot extra time to think about questions you hadn't anticipated.

UNDERSTAND EACH QUESTION COMPLETELY

There are few things more annoying than getting an exam returned with comments like, "Good essay, but you've written on the wrong topic" or "You didn't answer the question that was asked."

It's vital that you know exactly what the instructor is asking.

- **Underline the key words or phrases** in the questions that describe what is being asked for.
- **Don't just repeat** what's been written when you are asked to explain.
- **Don't just define** when you are asked to discuss. This is particularly important when questions themselves are long and complicated.

▶ How to Write a Good Essay

Let's take things step by step, beginning with a sample question.

Define and give examples of business franchises. Discuss the risks and benefits of these kinds of businesses. Describe the factors that will determine the future of franchising.

1. **Confine yourself to the question.** Limit your discussion just to what is required by the key words or phrases of the question.
2. **Make a time frame for the test.** When you first look at the test, do what you do in any test: Figure out how much time you will have to complete each question. Note how much each question is worth and write next to the question in the margin how much time you will spend on the question.

   The general rule is to spend one half of the time allotted to a question to planning the answer—by outline or map—and one half to the actual writing of the answer. For example:

   Question #1, 20 minutes total—ten minutes to plan, ten minutes to write.

Just Answer the Question

Don't write everything you know about a subject when you are only asked for specific information. Keep to the question. It is very tempting to put in lots of facts if you happen to know a good deal about the topic. The instructor, however, does not want to spend time reading extra material and will want to read only what's specifically required by the question.

---

3. **Make a map or outline of every answer.** As you read each question, jot down all the facts you can remember about the subject right away. Write them in the margin of the test book. After you have assessed how much you will say and how long you will take to say it, be sure to get that information down in a form you can follow. Outline or map the information you want to use to answer each question so that you have a visual image of all the facts or opinions you want to include in your answer.

▶ STRUCTURING YOUR ESSAY

THE THESIS STATEMENT

Start your essay by restating the question as your thesis statement. A thesis statement is a preview of the main ideas you will develop in the essay. Get in as many of the key words from the question in your thesis statement as you can. Here's an example:

> Franchises, defined as businesses such as Carvel or McDonald's™, that are authorized to offer a product or service owned by a parent company, offer both risks and rewards to the business owner.

CHOOSE A FORMAT

Decide upon how you will structure the answer to each question. You can simply restate your map or outline in paragraph form. Or you can organize it by one of the patterns that work well in essay tests: pros and cons, comparisons or contrasts, and opinions with reasons.

Each segment of your outline or map should be a separate paragraph that is introduced by a topic sentence. A topic sentence is a summary of the details that follow in the paragraph. Here's an example of a flow chart–style map:

Then, proceed to translate that map into an essay answer by writing your thesis statement. Follow that with two paragraphs, focusing each of them on one of the elements of your map.

Franchises, defined as businesses such as Carvel or McDonald's™, that are authorized to offer a product or service owned by a parent company, offer both risks and benefits to the business owner. (**thesis statement**)

First, let's look at the three main benefits of franchising. (**topic sentence**) The first of these is name recognition, which is helpful in marketing a known product. Second, a franchise offers a uniform and widely known product. Finally, there are low operating costs made possible by the parent companies.

On the other hand, there are risks to running franchise businesses. (**topic sentence**) Franchise businesses do not have the independence to alter the products or services to suit individual markets. Franchisees are also at the mercy of the corporate health of the parent company. If the parent company is doing poorly because of mismanagement in one part of the country, all franchises are compromised.

▶ WRITING THE ESSAY

Make your writing style suit the occasion.

- **Be concise and precise.** Keep your sentences short and simple, and don't pad your answer by repeating the same idea in different ways. Always be as *specific* as possible in making the points you want to make.
- **Use enumeration.** Introduce the points you want to make by using labeling words such as, "There are *three* major advantages to franchise businesses. The *first advantage* of these is name recognition."
- **Use signaling words.** Signal words, or transitions, guide your reader through your essay. These include words and phrases such as:

To begin with	However
Next	Consequently
Therefore	In conclusion

- **Avoid nonstandard forms or trendy idioms.** Don't use nonstandard forms in test essay writing.

Jane Jacobs tells it like it is when she talks about life in the "hood."

Not everyone (including perhaps the person marking your test) will know what the expression *life in the hood* means. A better way of writing it is:

Jane Jacobs tells some hard truths about life in urban neighborhoods.

- **Refer to authors and people of note by their last names.**

Jacobs [not Jane] believes that urban planning has ignored the importance of neighborhood life in the development of the city.

- **Keep your handwriting as legible as possible.** It may be difficult to make your words and sentences clear when you are rushing to finish on time. Have pity on the person who must read a stack of papers, each with a different style of handwriting. A neat and easy-to-read paragraph or essay is welcomed— and often rewarded—by the instructor.
- **Leave space between essays.** Skip a line or two so that you have some blank space should you want to add information that comes to mind later.

▶ IF WHAT YOU STUDIED ISN'T ON THE TEST

You have a great answer but no question to go with it! Don't beat yourself up for making wrong assumptions. Don't be hard on yourself for believing your classmate. (*Somebody told me Professor Jones always asks a question on the development of the trade union movement.*) If it happens to you, here are a couple of suggestions:

- Try to match up some of the information you predicted with what has been asked. You may not remember all the important information about the franchising business, but some of the information you prepared about unions may have some relevance to the franchising question.
- Put all the information you can recall about the subject at the beginning of your essay. Do as much as you can with what little you remember. Take special care that what information you have is well presented. You may get points for presentation if not for content.

▶ AT THE END OF THE TEST

Proofread your essays for spelling, grammar, and punctuation. Make sure you have capital letters and periods at the beginnings and ends of sentences. Write over corrected words carefully.

Compare your answers against your outlines or maps to make sure you have picked up every point you planned to make on the test. If you see that you left out something important, write it below the question or, if you didn't leave extra room on your paper, in the margin.

Look at your answers critically. Pretend you are the instructor who is reading the essays. What would you think of your work?

Be sure your name is on every test booklet. Many essay tests require several test booklets (usually called *blue books* though they come in many colors). Booklets can get separated during the grading process, so be sure each one you use has your name and that all books are fitted together (second and third booklets inside the first) before you hand the whole batch in to the instructor or proctor.

▶ IF YOU FEEL YOU'VE BEEN GRADED UNFAIRLY

In spite of all your preparation, you may get an exam back that carries a disappointing grade. If that happens, it is natural for you to be upset. The first person you want to blame, of course, is the instructor. It's easy to jump to the conclusion that he or she made mistakes in grading your paper. But here's what you should do instead:

- **Read over your paper carefully.** It is possible that the instructor accidentally skipped one of your essays or added the points incorrectly. Check out these possibilities first.
- **Read over your paper critically.** If you don't find some obvious reason for the low grade, see how it sounds to you now. Did you show what you knew in the most organized, clearest, most concise, most accurate way possible? Read the instructor's comments. Try to understand the instructor's criticisms.
- **Confront your teacher cordially.** If you are still convinced that you deserve a better grade, make an appointment to see the instructor. Approach the instructor with an attitude of inquiry. Explain that you want to know how to prepare more successfully for the next test. Bring your test and written questions about the test to discuss. Really listen to what the instructor says about the test. Learn from your mistakes before the next exam.

On the following page, try out your essay-writing ability by making a time plan and writing the answers for a short-essay exam.

IN SHORT

You can express your knowledge clearly and convincingly in an essay test by organizing your answer before you begin to write it out. Spend half the allotted time planning your answer by outlining or mapping and the other half of your time writing the answer itself. Read all of the questions before you answer any of them and remember to write legibly!

PRACTICING ESSAY ANSWERS

In 45 minutes, answer each of the following questions in a well-developed paragraph. Before you begin, decide and note how long you plan to spend on each question based on its point value. Use the following space to outline or map your answers. Write the essay answers on separate sheets of paper.

1. Explain the need for a diet and exercise plan before taking a major test. Give examples of good diet and exercise habits. (30 points) _____ min.
2. Identify three learning modalities, or styles, and tell how a student would use each modality to aid in test preparation. (30 points) _____ min.
3. Discuss the similarities and differences between studying for a standardized test and studying for a classroom test. (40 points) _____ min.

PRACTICING ESSAY ANSWERS

(Completed sample)

1. In order to do your best on a test, you must pay attention to the diet and exercise your body needs to do its best. **(thesis statement)** Good health that comes from nutritious foods and regular exercise helps you to concentrate, combat fatigue, and avoid illness during the stress of studying over long periods of time.

As you prepare to take a major test, be careful to maintain a healthy, well-balanced diet. **(topic sentence)** Stay away from salty snacks or processed foods that contain extra salt. Limit your intake of coffee and soda. Try not to order out prepared foods very often. Keep regular mealtimes instead of grazing during the day.

During test preparation, your body also needs regular exercise to offset long hours spent sitting at your desk. **(topic sentence)** Be sure to do some form of aerobic exercise at least three times a week. Take walks to rest from study several times a day. Make an effort to participate in vigorous exercise through team sports or individual activities such as swimming, jogging, or biking.

2. No two people learn exactly alike. Everyone has a unique learning style. There are three specific styles by which people learn. **(thesis statement)** These are the visual, the auditory, and the kinesthetic, or tactile, modalities.

People who learn best visually like to see what they need to learn. **(topic sentence)** Visual learners should color-code important information. They should map or outline information from their textbooks to get a strong visual cue for memorizing. They should pay special attention to pictures, maps, charts, and other visual references while they read.

People who learn best by listening are auditory learners. **(topic sentence)** They should read aloud to themselves or others. They should tape-record notes and play them back during study sessions. Auditory learners also benefit from working with a study group in which they can hear the views of other students.

Kinesthetic, or tactile, learners learn by interacting physically with the text. **(topic sentence)** They should take lots of notes and underline or highlight text as they read. Some kinesthetic learners are helped by copying or recopying class notes or notes from the textbook.

3. There are both similarities and differences in the methods for studying for occasional tests such as the GED and those needed to prepare for a classroom test. **(thesis statement)**

There are two important ways in which preparation for a standardized test is similar to preparing for a class test. **(topic sentence)** First, you need a systematic and organized study plan. Second, you need to develop the learning strategies that will allow you to study effectively.

Students must also realize, however, that there are distinct differences between preparing for classroom and standardized tests. **(topic sentence)** Classroom tests contain a wider variety of questions. Standardized tests are mostly multiple choice. Class tests are designed to reflect the specific instructor's interests and expertise. Standardized tests do not offer the opportunity to anticipate the questions the instructor is likely to include on the test.

It's not just what you say, it's also how you say it. In this chapter, you'll learn how to improve the basic writing skills you need to have to score well on essay tests.

Writing Basics for the Essay Test

The content of your essay answer is certainly important, but so is the language you use to convey that information. That's why this entire chapter is devoted to how to make your extended-answer questions well organized, clear, concise, and accurate.

▶ HOW TO WRITE IN AN ORGANIZED WAY

Outline or map your essay first. These visual strategies for organizing information before you start to write are very helpful. They're the quickest way for you to get your ideas down on paper. When you first open your test, you should spend *one half* of whatever time you decide to spend on the question in making a map or outline of what you have to say.

Following are some organizing diagrams that can be used to set up your essay before you start writing.

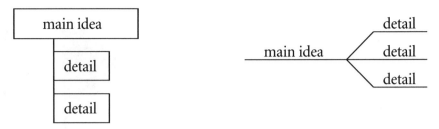

Flow chart:

Ladder:

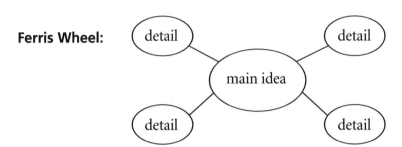

Ferris Wheel:

► EXPRESSING YOURSELF CLEARLY

USE THE SPECIFIC VOCABULARY OF YOUR SUBJECT

It's a good idea to be prepared with the words (properly spelled!) that pertain to the subject of the essay question. As you study, write down the words you think are important to the subject on note cards.

For example, in a course in economics, you should know the following words:

annuities	margins
deficits	discount rates
equities	

For a course in English literature, you would want to know terms such as:

imagery	irony
exposition	symbolism
narrative	genre

You should also be prepared to cite specific names of characters, authors, acts, laws, theories, and important people in your subject areas.

BEWARE OF EASILY CONFUSED WORDS AND TERMS

Here are some terms used in essay writing that are often misused because they sound or look alike.

Term	Meaning	Example
illusion	a misleading impression	He had no *illusions* about her feelings.
allusion	a reference to a commonly known source	The biblical *allusion* was good.
advise	to give counsel (verb)	I *advise* you to study hard.
advice	a recommendation (noun)	Dad gave me good *advice*.
principle	a basic truth or law	The *principle* of truth in advertising was challenged by the tobacco companies.
principal	the head of a school	The new *principal* addressed the sixth grade assembly.
affect	to influence (verb)	Her injury did not *affect* her performance.
effect	the result of an action (noun)	Her childhood trauma had an enormous *effect* on her life.
farther	a greater distance	He can skate *farther* than his sister.
further	in addition	There will be no *further* discussion until the attorney arrives.
quote	to cite someone else's language (verb)	He liked to *quote* his father's wise advice.
quotation	the citation of someone's work	He included numerous *quotations* of scientific studies in his monograph.
lose	to misplace something (verb)	He didn't want to *lose* the election.
loose	unattached(adjective)	He was considered a *loose* cannon, who couldn't be controlled by Congress.

BE AWARE OF THE DIFFERENT FLAVORS OF WORDS

Many words that people use in writing have both denotations and connotations. This means that words have meanings or feelings—*connotations*—that go beyond their dictionary definitions—their *denotations*. Thus, words have different *flavors*, depending on their use in a sentence.

The words *fat, obese, chubby,* and *plump* all suggest that someone is overweight. However, we associate *chubbiness* and *plumpness* with appealing images of babies and small children, while words like *obese* and *fat* call up mental pictures of unattractive, heavy grownups.

If you were describing a particular human behavior, for instance, you may think about the difference in the images suggested by the word *aggressive* as opposed to the flavor of the word *assertive.* Which word best expresses the attitude you observed?

► WRITING CONCISELY

KEEP SENTENCE STRUCTURE SIMPLE

The basic subject-verb-object sentence structure is always safe to use in an essay test. It will be boring for your instructor to read, however, if you don't vary the sentence structure somewhat.

Pare Down Long Clauses to Words and Phrases

Less is often better. For example, you could write:

> The hero, who was dashing and romantic in the early part of the book, turned out to be the villain in the end.

However, the following sentence is cleaner and stronger:

> The romantic hero was later revealed to be the villain.

Use Strong Verbs

Get in the habit of using meaningful verbs. For example, look at this sentence:

> The social worker is charged with supervising and writing reports on 30 clients a week.

More meaningful verbs would make the sentence look like this:

> The social worker supervises and reports on 30 clients a week.

Always use active voice instead of passive whenever possible. Here is the passive:

> Firefighters have been instructed by their superiors to open all vents in the room before removing the flammable substance.

Here is the active voice:

> Supervisors have instructed firefighters to open all vents before removing the flammable substance.

KEEP THE LANGUAGE CLEAN AND CLEAR

Get yourself accustomed to writing in a straightforward way. You can be expressive and convincing without the help of unnecessary adverbs, adjectives, and extra clauses.

Leave Out Unnecessary Words or Phrases

The italicized words in the next two sentences aren't essential; they just take up space—and take extra time to read:

> *It has been said that* we all bear responsibility for the actions of our government. *It would seem certain that* the new Congress will bring about badly needed reforms.

Don't Repeat Yourself

Be careful not to say the same thing twice in two different ways. For example, in the following two sentences, one set of italicized words should be taken out to avoid repetition.

> He had no idea how to solve the *troublesome* problem *that was bothering him.*
> *At this point in time*, he feels that action should be taken *now.*

Don't Try to Make It Sound Fancy

Very informal language has no place in essay test answers. And neither does overly formal or elaborate language. Don't use a long, complicated word or expression when a simple one will do equally well. For instance:

> The facilitator in the learning station will offer positive reinforcement to the learner.

That sentence is better written as the following:

The instructor in the classroom will give the student a pat on the back.

▶ AVOIDING LANGUAGE MISTAKES

One of the challenges of writing essay answers for a test is that it has to be done within a time limit. When you feel pressured by the clock, it's easy to be sloppy in the so-called mechanics of writing—the spelling, grammar, and usage skills—that are essential in a good essay answer. And during a test, you don't have access to the computer's spell-checker or grammar checker!

There's no room here for a detailed review of spelling and grammar skills—just examples of the kinds of errors to avoid because they *show*. These are the mistakes that detract from your writing. They stand out and take the spotlight away from the good ideas you may have expressed.

DON'T COMMIT ANY MAJOR USAGE ERRORS

Here are the top ten errors that mess up your writing.

Error	Rule	Example
Don't confuse *its* and *it's*.	*It's* is a contraction meaning *it is*. Its is a possessive pronoun.	*It's* a long journey. Virtue is *its* own reward.
Don't confuse *fewer* with *less* and *amount* with *number*.	*Fewer* and *number* are used with things you can specifically count. *Amount* and *less* are used with things you can't specifically count.	There are *fewer* calories in soda. We gave to a large *number* of charities. We have *less* time to relax. He had a large *amount* of cash.
Don't use *of* for *have*.	*Should of* and *would of* are incorrect.	I *should have* gone alone. I *would have* eaten earlier.

Error	Rule	Example
Don't say *use to* and *suppose to*.	*Used to* and *supposed to* are correct.	I *used to* work at Macy's. He was *supposed to* go to the game.
Don't say *the reason why is because*	You are saying the same thing twice. Rephrase the sentence.	I said Judy was in camp *because* I thought it was true.
Don't confuse *their*, *there*, and *they're*.	*There* is an adverb telling where. *They're* is a contraction for *they are*. *Their* is a possessive pronoun.	Put it over *there*. *They're* going to the movies. They wore *their* coats.
Never say *is when* or *is where*.	These are unnecessarily wordy phrases.	Mapping *is* a diagram of ideas in writing. (*not* Mapping is when you diagram your ideas in writing.)
Don't confuse subjects and verbs.	Make subjects and verbs agree.	*John*, along with his sister Jane, *has* a long commute to school.
Rewrite sentence to make pronouns match their nouns.	Don't use a plural pronoun when you are trying to be gender neutral.	Everyone go to *their* seats should be They will go to *their* own seats.
Don't confuse *to*, *two*, and *too*.	*To* is a preposition. *Too* means also. *Two* is a number.	She is going *to* school. Her brother is going, *too*. They will take *two* buses.

WATCH FOR MAJOR GRAMMATICAL ERRORS

Avoid the big grammar mistakes that can drive instructors to early retirement.

- Underline (or italicize when you're using a computer) titles of books, magazines, films, plays, musical compositions, and newspapers: In an article in the *New York Times* . . .
- Put quotes around titles of poems, short stories, and titles of magazine articles: In the short story, "Paul's Case" . . .
- Capitalize proper nouns—names, places, languages, historical epochs, official course titles, organizations, political parties, and titles: Thomas Jefferson is considered to be the father of the Democratic Party. Make sure your capitals look like capitals!
- Use periods, question marks, or exclamation points at the ends of sentences.
- Don't use apostrophes for plurals: He had two exams (not *exam's*) on the same day.
- Don't use quotation marks for emphasis: He wanted to go to "gym," not the park, after lunch. This sentence is not correct; there is no reason to use quotation marks here.

DON'T MAKE SPELLING ERRORS

Sound out words in your mind if you are not sure how to spell them. Remember that long vowels inside words are usually followed by single consonants: *sofa, total*. Short vowels inside words are usually followed by double consonants: *dribble, scissors*.

Give yourself auditory listening clues when you learn words. Say *Wed-nes-day* or *lis-ten* or *bus-i-ness* to yourself when you spell so that you remember to add the letters you don't hear.

Look at each part of the word. See if there is a root, prefix, or suffix that will always be spelled the same way. For example, in *uninhabitable, un, in,* and *able* are always spelled the same way. What is left is *habit,* a self-contained word that is not difficult to spell.

Check your command of the English language by correcting the sentences on the next page.

IN SHORT

You can present your ideas in a well-organized and concise way while writing an answer to an essay question. Avoid making glaring language mistakes by reviewing basic grammar and spelling rules before the test. Keep your sentence structure simple but varied.

TEST YOUR LANGUAGE SMARTS

Rewrite the following sentences to correct errors in mechanics or usage.

1. Their are many reasons why you should outline your essay before you write.

_____

_____

2. The speaker used excellent quotes that had a great affect on his audience.

_____

_____

3. They should of gone too they're counselor's before leaving school that day.

_____

_____

4. According to the New York Times, less students are enrolling in ROTC programs now than in the 1980s.

_____

_____

5. Economically disadvantaged persons have difficulty remitting their revenue enhancements.

_____

_____

6. A parent often has only their common sense to rely on.

_____

_____

7. The hard working employee was very diligent.

_____

_____

8. I was told by the IRS that my "refund" would be late.

_____

_____

9. In my considered opinion "The Great Gatsby," a novel by F. Scott Fitzgerald, is the most significant book to be written in the twentieth century.

_____

_____

10. FDR took a lot of heat with his lend lease act prior two our getting involved with WW2.

_____

_____

TEST YOUR LANGUAGE SMARTS

(Completed sample)

1. Their are many reasons why you should outline your essay before you write.

There are many reasons for outlining your essays before you write.

2. The speaker used excellent quotes that had a great affect on his audience.

The speaker used excellent quotations that had a great effect on his audience.

3. They should of gone too they're counselor's before leaving school that day.

They should have gone to their counselors before leaving school that day.

4. According to the New York Times, less students are enrolling in ROTC programs now than in the 1980s.

According to the <u>New York Times</u>, fewer students are enrolling in ROTC programs now than in the 1980s.

5. Economically disadvantaged persons have difficulty remitting their revenue enhancements.

Low-income people have trouble paying their taxes.

6. A parent often has only their common sense to rely on.

Parents often must rely only on their common sense.

7. The hard working employee was very diligent.

He was a hard-working employee.

8. I was told by the IRS that my "refund" would be late.

The IRS notified me that my refund would be late.

9. In my considered opinion "The Great Gatsby," a novel by F. Scott Fitzgerald, is the most significant book to be written in the twentieth century.

I believe that Fitzgerald's <u>The Great Gatsby</u> is the twentieth century's best novel.

10. FDR took a lot of heat with his lend lease act prior two our getting involved with WW2.

Many were critical of the Lend Lease Act proposed by President Roosevelt before the United States' entry into World War II.

IN THIS CHAPTER, YOU'LL PRACTICE TAKING A TEST MODELED ON STANDARDIZED TESTS SUCH AS THE GED. USE THE STRATEGIES HERE THAT YOU'VE LEARNED FOR ANSWERING MULTIPLE-CHOICE QUESTIONS.

Test Yourself: A Practice Standardized Test

This sample test is designed to take approximately one hour. The best idea is for you to complete the whole exam in one sitting, although you can break it up so that you complete one-third of the test at a time for 20 minutes a day for three days.

Remember to take a few minutes to preview the entire test, so you know what's in store for you before you start answering questions.

PART I: VOCABULARY

Choose the word that means the same or nearly the same as the underlined word.

1. a <u>gregarious</u> person
   a. fearful
   b. sociable
   c. comical
   d. generous

2. an <u>obsolete</u> attitude
   a. modern
   b. hostile
   c. outdated
   d. welcoming

3. an <u>innocuous</u> statement
   a. harmless
   b. hateful
   c. scripted
   d. public

Choose the word or phrase that most nearly means the opposite of the underlined word.

4. to show <u>antipathy</u> for
   a. friendship
   b. ill-feeling
   c. concern
   d. disdain

5. An <u>arrogant</u> manner is
   a. courtly.
   b. angry.
   c. annoying.
   d. humble.

6. <u>Impulsive</u> actions are
   a. spur of the moment.
   b. cautious.
   c. joyous.
   d. fast.

Choose the word that best completes each of the following sentences.

7. The _____ smells coming from the kitchen reminded her that she hadn't eaten all day.
   a. bitter
   b. tantalizing
   c. unpleasant
   d. sickening

8. He wrote under a _____ because he didn't want anyone to know his identity.
   a. disability
   b. pseudonym
   c. tree
   d. mask

9. Because he wished to be anonymous, the family was never to know the name of their _____.
   a. lawyer
   b. judge
   c. mortician
   d. benefactor

10. Despite her disability, the girl never let her blindness be a(n) _____ to her success.
   a. asset
   b. hindrance
   c. encouragement
   d. scapegoat

PART II: SPELLING

Choose the word that is spelled correctly and best completes each of the following sentences.

11. The officer's handwriting was _____.
   a. illegible
   b. ilegible
   c. ineligible
   d. ileggible

12. It's nobody's _____ if you want to study ten hours over the weekend.
   a. bussness
   b. busness
   c. bisness
   d. business

13. Although he was not in the mood to cook dinner, he did not want to appear _____.
   a. inhospitable
   b. unhospital
   c. inhospittable
   d. inhospitible

14. The scientists had found that _____ viruses caused the illness.
   a. muttant
   b. mutent
   c. mutant
   d. myutant

15. She had many _____ works available at her desk.
   a. refference
   b. referrance
   c. referance
   d. reference

PART III: LANGUAGE MECHANICS

Choose the answer that shows the best punctuation for the underlined part of sentences 16–20.

16. Did you see an article in the *Chief-Leader* <u>about an upcoming test for the Police department exam.</u>
   a. about an upcoming test for the Police Department exam.
   b. about an upcoming test for the police department exam.
   c. about an upcoming test for the Police department exam?
   d. about an upcoming test for the police department exam?
   e. correct as it is

17. <u>Its a shame that professor Smith</u> never achieved tenure at the university.

    a. Its a shame that Professor Smith

    b. It's a shame that professor Smith

    c. Its a shame, that Professor Smith

    d. It's a shame that Professor Smith

    e. correct as it is

18. "<u>Look out theres a tornado coming</u>" said the weather expert.

    a. "Look out! There's a tornado coming"

    b. "Look out. Theres a tornado coming."

    c. "Look out! Theres a tornado coming!"

    d. "Look out! There's a tornado coming,"

    e. correct as it is

19. <u>Although I had to go to school early,</u> I stayed up long past bedtime.

    a. Although I had to go to school early

    b. Although I had to go to school early:

    c. Although I had to go to school early—

    d. Although, I had to go to school early

    e. correct as it is

20. <u>Its to late to hand in</u> the assignment now.

    a. It's to late to hand in

    b. It's too late too hand in

    c. Its too late to hand in

    d. It's too late to hand in

    e. correct as it is

PART IV: LANGUAGE EXPRESSION

Choose the word or phrase that best completes each of the following sentences.

21. They went to _____ house to pick up a change of clothes.

    a. their

    b. they're

    c. there

    d. they

22. She had collected a large _____ of awards in her long career.
- **a.** number
- **b.** amount
- **c.** type
- **d.** kind

23. The police cruiser responded to an incident that _____ at the corner of Third and Main streets.
- **a.** is breaking out
- **b.** had broke out
- **c.** was broke out
- **d.** had broken out

24. There are _____ murders in New York City this year than last year.
- **a.** less
- **b.** fewer
- **c.** smaller
- **d.** larger

25. The woman _____ made the quilt was an experienced seamstress.
- **a.** that
- **b.** whom
- **c.** who
- **d.** which

PART V: MATH

26. $400 \times 76 =$
- **a.** 52,000
- **b.** 30,100
- **c.** 20,400
- **d.** 3,040
- **e.** none of these

27. $52{,}834 \div 9 =$

    a. 5,870 R4

    b. 5,826 R2

    c. 5,826

    d. 5,871

    e. none of these

28. $4\frac{1}{5} + 1\frac{2}{5} + 3\frac{3}{10} =$

    a. $9\frac{1}{10}$

    b. $8\frac{9}{10}$

    c. $8\frac{4}{5}$

    d. $8\frac{6}{15}$

    e. none of these

29. $\frac{1}{6} + \frac{7}{12} + \frac{2}{3} =$

    a. $\frac{10}{24}$

    b. $2\frac{1}{6}$

    c. $1\frac{5}{6}$

    d. $1\frac{5}{12}$

    e. none of these

30. $426 - 7.2 =$

    a. 354.0

    b. 425.28

    c. 418.8

    d. 41.88

    e. none of these

31. Which is another way to write $\frac{4}{25}$?

    a. 4%

    b. 16%

    c. 40%

    d. 100%

32. A piece of ribbon 3 feet 4 inches long is divided in 5 equal parts. How long is each part?
  a. 1 foot 2 inches
  b. 10 inches
  c. 8 inches
  d. 6 inches

33. A snack machine accepts only quarters. Candy bars cost 25¢ each, packages of peanuts cost 75¢ each, and cans of cola cost 50¢ each. How many quarters are needed to buy two candy bars, one package of peanuts, and one can of cola?
  a. 5
  b. 6
  c. 7
  d. 8

34. The perimeter of a rectangle is 148 feet. Its two longest sides add up to 86 feet. What is the length of each of its two shortest sides?
  a. 31 ft.
  b. 42 ft.
  c. 62 ft.
  d. 74 ft.

PART VI: READING COMPREHENSION

Read the following paragraphs and answer the questions that follow.

Since the mid-1980s, there has been considerable controversy over whether college curriculums should continue to offer the so-called core curriculum. Primarily, the core courses consisted of mandatory classes in Western history and culture and were intended to form a common foundation of learning for the education of all students. The literature of these courses is commonly referred to as the literary canon. However, college campuses became more ethnically diverse as a result of open enrollments and affirmative action initiatives in the late 1960s and 1970s. As a result, there were increased demands for college programs to reflect that diversity by the inclusion of programs in ethnic studies and by the abandonment of many literary works that had previously comprised the canon. Feminists, too, called for more study of the works of women authors and accused colleges of limiting their study to the writings of Dead White European Males or DWEMs. Ironically, the call for the end of the canon came just as core courses were being reinstated on many campuses after years of being discarded in favor of programs that were seen as more relevant to modern life. This movement back to the core was largely in response to critics, such as E. D. Hirsch and Alan Bloom, who believe that a shared body of knowledge that is represented by the works in the traditional literary canon is necessary to provide a shared cultural literacy for educated people.

35. The main idea of this paragraph is
   a. colleges should abandon the core curriculum.
   b. core courses exclude women.
   c. colleges are examining the role of core courses in their curricula.
   d. core courses are open only to European men.

36. In this paragraph, the word *mandatory* most nearly means
   a. outdated.
   b. optional.
   c. required.
   d. difficult.

37. Bloom and Hirsch believe that the core curriculum
   a. should be eliminated.
   b. should be optional.
   c. should be required.
   d. should be more inclusive.

38. The author suggests in this paragraph that
   a. works by DWEMs should be eliminated from the core curriculum.
   b. the traditional literary canon is outdated.
   c. colleges should be more inclusive.
   d. works by DWEMs are seen as irrelevant to the experience of women and minorities.

Considerable national attention has focused in recent years on the failure of city, state, and national agencies to protect the lives and welfare of children. The public outrage that followed high-profile child abuse cases has meant that more and more children are being taken into foster care to protect them from endangerment in their own homes. This has meant that already overburdened caseworkers are given even larger workloads, as they try to cope with the flood of children remanded into care by the courts. In several large cities where the numbers of children threaten to overwhelm the systems designated to provide care, a number of reforms have been instituted to assist them. Among the most promising is the effort to site services in communities rather than at distant social service agencies. Wherever possible, children are being placed with relatives or with foster families in their home communities. Thus, they are not removed from the neighborhood, extended family, and school connections that serve them well. Caseloads have been reduced for many social service workers, and workers are being recruited from the communities that have the greatest need. Social service agencies are insisting upon a uniform database regarding foster care cases that can be accessed by all those charged with the supervision of children in care. In this way, fewer children can fall through bureaucratic cracks when files are lost or children are moved from one location to another. Sibling groups, too, are kept together as often as possible so that children can maintain family relationships while in foster care.

39. The best title for this paragraph would be
   a. "The High Cost of Child Abuse."
   b. "Child Abuse: A National Scandal."
   c. "Community-Based Social Work: Helping the Foster System Work."
   d. "The Risks and Benefits of Foster Care."

40. In this paragraph, the word *siblings* refers to
   a. extended family.
   b. community groups.
   c. foster parents.
   d. brothers and sisters.

41. Computer access to records is important to social workers so that they can
   a. learn about a child's medical history.
   b. keep track of progress on a child's case.
   c. keep personal information out of the hands of other social workers.
   d. improve computer skills.

42. In this paragraph, the author suggests that
   a. in the past, social workers were given little assistance.
   b. social workers are lazy.
   c. social workers need to take more responsibility.
   d. community connections are important to good social work.

A Narrow Fellow in the Grass
by Emily Dickinson

A narrow fellow in the grass
Occasionally rides;
You may have met him—did you not?
His notice sudden is.

The grass divides as with a comb,
A spotted shaft is seen;
And then it closes at your feet
And opens further on.

He likes a boggy acre,
A floor too cool for corn.
Yet when a boy, and barefoot,
I more than once, at morn,

Have passed, I thought, a whip-lash
Unbraiding in the sun—
When, stooping to secure it,
It wrinkled, and was gone.

Several of nature's people
I know, and they know me;
I feel for them a transport
Of cordiality;

But never met this fellow,
Attended or alone,
Without a tighter breathing,
And zero at the bone.

43. Who or what is the *fellow* in this poem?
   a. a whip-lash
   b. a weed
   c. a snake
   d. a gust of wind

44. The phrase "Without a tighter breathing / And zero at the bone" most nearly means
   a. without being frightened.
   b. without counting steps.
   c. without wearing shoes.
   d. without running away.

45. The phrase *nature's people* means
   a. campers.
   b. environmentalists.
   c. animals.
   d. vegetarians.

46. This poem is most likely set in
   a. Massachusetts.
   b. winter.
   c. autumn.
   d. summer.

47. The speaker of this poem is most likely
   a. an adult woman.
   b. an adult man.
   c. a young girl.
   d. a zookeeper.

In the twenty-first century, when African-American athletes compete in and often dominate nearly every competitive sport, it is difficult to realize that a mere 50 years ago the appearance of a single African-American man on a baseball team was a revolutionary event. When Jackie Robinson joined the Brooklyn Dodgers in 1947, he was the first man of his race to play in the major leagues in this country. Although the all-African-American Negro Leagues had nourished talented players for years, none had been allowed to play on a team with a national following. After World War II, the gradual but persistent initiatives by many African-Americans to gain their civil rights meant that it was only a matter of time before our national pastime would be challenged to include players of color. Recruited by Branch Rickey, the general manager of the Dodgers, Jackie Robinson, former football star at the University of California at Los Angeles, finally donned the Dodger uniform. In the beginning, Robinson had to withstand the hostility of some fans and fellow players and was subjected to their insulting and often dangerous behavior. He met their insults with dignity, however, and went on to lead his team to six National League pennants and a triumphant defeat of the Yankees in the 1955 World Series. He was elected to the Baseball Hall of Fame in 1962. Despite the pioneering efforts of Rickey, Robinson, and others, it still took many years before all teams were integrated. However, it was their courage and tenacity that allowed baseball to lead other sports to open their ranks to African-American athletes and to change the face of American games forever.

48. Which of the following best describes the subject of this passage?
   a. the life of Jackie Robinson
   b. racial discrimination in baseball
   c. Robinson's role in integrating baseball
   d. insulting behavior at baseball games

49. In this paragraph, the word *pioneering* most nearly means
   a. dangerous.
   b. refreshing.
   c. triumphant.
   d. unprecedented.

50. When Robinson first played with the Dodgers,
   a. he was welcomed as a hero.
   b. he was paid less than other players.
   c. he was subjected to insults and threats.
   d. he defied the orders of Branch Rickey.

Check your answers on this practice test with the *Standardized Test Answers and Explanations* that follow. Note what questions you missed. Plan to spend some time reviewing those areas in which your performance was weak.

▶ STANDARDIZED TEST ANSWERS AND EXPLANATIONS

PART I: VOCABULARY
   1. b. *Gregarious* means *sociable*.
   2. c. *Obsolete* means *outdated*.
   3. a. *Innocuous* means *harmless*.
   4. a. The opposite of *antipathy* (*dislike*) is *friendship*.

5. d. The opposite of *arrogant* is *humble*.

6. b. The opposite of *impulsive* is *cautious*.

7. b. Food would be a *tantalizing* (*tempting*) smell to someone who hasn't eaten.

8. b. *Pseudonym* means *false name*.

9. d. Only the *benefactor* could have been anonymous. All the others had to be known to the family.

10. b. Because the girl is successful, her blindness is not a *hindrance, or drawback*.

PART II: SPELLING

11. a. *illegible*

12. d. *business*

13. a. *inhospitable*

14. c. *mutant*

15. d. *reference*

PART III: LANGUAGE MECHANICS

16. d. A question needs a question mark, and *police department* does not need to be capitalized.

17. d. The contraction *it's* needs an apostrophe; Professor Smith is a title and requires a capital letter.

18. d. *Look out* is an exclamation, so it should be followed by an exclamation point. The contraction *there's* needs an apostrophe and should be capitalized as the beginning of the sentence; there is a comma after the quotation.

19. e. A comma should come before a clause that begins a sentence.

20. d. The contraction *It's* needs an apostrophe; the sentence requires the adverb *too*.

PART IV: LANGUAGE EXPRESSION

21. a. A possessive pronoun is needed.

22. a. Awards can be counted, so the correct word is *number*.

23. d. *Had broken out* matches the verb *responded*.

24. b. Murders can be counted, so the word needed is *fewer*.

25. c. Use the word *who* when referring to people as subjects.

PART V: MATH

26. e. The correct answer is 30,400.

27. a. If you got a different answer, you probably made an error in multiplication or subtraction.

28. b. Incorrect answers include adding both the numerator and the denominator and not converting fifths to tenths properly.

29. d. You have to convert all three fractions to twelfths before adding them.

30. c. The other answers were subtracted without aligning the decimal points.

31. b. Four divided by 25 equals 0.16, or 16%.

32. c. Three feet 4 inches equals 40 inches; 40 divided by 5 is 8.

33. c. Two candy bars require 2 quarters; one package of peanuts requires 3 quarters; one can of cola requires 2 quarters—for a total of 7 quarters.

34. a. The first step in solving the problem is to subtract 86 from 148. The remainder, 62, is then divided by 2.

PART VI: READING COMPREHENSION

35. c. The main idea is the debate over the canon, which means that colleges must examine their own attitudes about the core curriculum.

36. c. The meaning of *mandatory* as *required* is signaled by the reference to the core as being the "common foundation of learning for the education of all students."

37. c. The clue to this answer lies in the sentence that says that Bloom and Hirsch believe that the canon is "necessary to provide a shared cultural literacy for educated people."

38. d. This is implied by the reference to objections both by minorities and by women to the core curriculum.

39. c. The title of the passage should relate to the main idea that community-based services are needed to help with the rising numbers of children in foster care.

40. d. Siblings are brothers and sisters. The clue here is in the reference to family relationships.

41. b. This detail is in the reference to files being lost and children changing locations while in foster care.

42. d. It is implied throughout the passage that community resources are important to the efficient delivery of child welfare services.

43. c. The *fellow* frightens the speaker, according to the last stanza. In the fourth stanza, the speaker describes seeing something that looks like a whip-lash but then moves away. A snake is the only one of the four choices that could fit these criteria.

44. a. *Tighter breathing* indicates fear, as does *zero at the bone,* because one is sometimes said to be *cold with fear.*

45. c. There are no campers, environmentalists, or vegetarians in the poem.

46. d. The grass in the first two stanzas, the sun in the fourth stanza, and the speaker's bare feet in the third stanza suggest summertime.

47. b. The third stanza contains the phrase *when a boy,* implying that the speaker was a boy in the past and is now, therefore, an adult man.

48. c. This is the most general statement and is, therefore, the best statement of the subject.

49. d. *Pioneering* implies something that had not been experienced before; therefore, *unprecedented* makes the most sense here.

50. c. This detail is revealed in the sentence "...had to withstand the hostility of some fans and fellow players and was subjected to their insulting and often dangerous behavior."

HOW WELL DID I DO ON THE PRACTICE STANDARDIZED TEST? A SELF-ANALYSIS

I answered ___/10 questions correctly in the Vocabulary section.

I answered ___/5 questions correctly in the Spelling section.

I answered ___/5 questions correctly in the Language Mechanics section.

I answered ___/5 questions correctly in the Language Expression section.

I answered ___/9 questions correctly in the Math section.

I answered ___/16 questions correctly in the Reading Comprehension section.

I answered the most questions correctly in the _____ section(s).

I think I did well in these sections because

I did not do as well in the _____ section(s).

I think I did not do as well in these sections because

To improve my performance in these sections, I need to

_____ review my basic skills (spelling, vocabulary, math, or grammar).

_____ read questions more carefully.

_____ select answers more carefully.

_____ work more quickly.

_____ work more slowly.

Other _____

_____

IN THIS CHAPTER, YOU WILL APPLY THE TEST-TAKING
STRATEGIES YOU'VE LEARNED IN THIS BOOK TO AN EXAM
YOU MIGHT FIND IN A CLASSROOM.

Test Yourself: A Practice Classroom Test

The exam that follows is based on what you have read in this book. It is, therefore, similar to many classroom tests that are based on textbook material. Like the test in Chapter 14, this sample test is longer than 20 minutes; it's designed to take 50 minutes. Your best bet is to vary the 20-minutes-a-day formula and take the full 50 minutes, so you can complete the test in one sitting. Be sure to preview the test and plan your time before you start!

PART I: IDENTIFICATIONS (10 POINTS)

Define or give examples of each of the following.

1. standardized test

_____

2. stems (in testing)

_____

3. mnemonics

_____

4. distributed practice

_____

5. graphic aids

_____

PART II: TRUE/FALSE (10 POINTS)

Mark ten of the following statements as true or false.

_____ **6.** *Connotation* refers to the dictionary definition of a word.

_____ **7.** The GED is an example of a classroom test.

_____ **8.** Distributed practice is best accomplished by cramming.

_____ **9.** A monthly calendar is generally more useful than a weekly calendar in scheduling study time.

_____ **10.** A study group should not have fewer than ten members.

_____ **11.** It is usually not a good idea to study in bed.

_____ **12.** You should spend the same amount of time planning your answer on an essay test as you spend writing the answer.

_____ **13.** *Visualization* refers to a learning modality.

_____ **14.** Procrastination is a method for curing test anxiety.

_____ **15.** It is usually better to use active voice in writing.

_____ **16.** The thesis statement is a review of all the facts in a paragraph.

_____ **17.** You should never play the radio while you are studying.

PART III: MULTIPLE CHOICE (10 POINTS)

Circle the correct answer in each of the following.

18. All of the following are true EXCEPT
  a. auditory learners learn best by listening.
  b. breaking lists into groups of six or any other even number makes them easier to memorize.
  c. annotating, outlining, and mapping study notes makes material easier to review.
  d. the most common type of memory trick is an acronym.

19. Instructors favor multiple-choice tests because
  a. they penalize those who have poor language skills.
  b. they are more time-consuming to write.
  c. they are more difficult.
  d. they allow testing of a wider range of skills.

20. When you look at the test for the first time, you should
  a. start working as soon as possible.
  b. do all of the essays first.
  c. listen carefully to the instructions.
  d. make sure you have pens and pencils.

21. Flash cards are preferable to notebook pages because
  a. they can contain more information.
  b. they are shorter.
  c. they are neater.
  d. they can be carried in your pocket or purse.

22. When answering true/false questions, you should
  a. usually choose false.
  b. read the statement very quickly to get a first impression.
  c. choose true if at least part of the statement is true.
  d. be wary of statements that contain absolutes, such as *always* and *never*.

23. Some multiple-choice questions include questions based on graphic material because
  a. graphics summarize large amounts of information in a small space.
  b. graphics are easier to write.
  c. graphics are more familiar to older students than to younger learners.
  d. graphic questions test listening skills.

24. The way to prevent the onset of test anxiety is to
   a. study at least three hours per day.
   b. pay attention to small problems.
   c. postpone a vigorous diet and exercise plan.
   d. keep a well-organized routine and a positive attitude.

25. A good place to locate information about standardized tests and test dates is
   a. the telephone book.
   b. the Internet.
   c. the classified ads in the newspapers.
   d. a course outline or syllabus.

26. When studying before sleep, you should
   a. allow at least 30 minutes between study and sleep.
   b. watch television to relax between study and sleep.
   c. allow no activity or interference between study and sleep.
   d. listen to the radio, but do not watch television between study and sleep.

27. A monthly calendar is preferable to a weekly calendar in organizing study time because
   a. it is more pleasing to the eye.
   b. it can hold more information.
   c. it can show clusters of exam activity more easily.
   d. it is smaller and easier to handle.

PART IV: COMPLETIONS (20 POINTS)

Complete the following sentences.

28. The word that refers to associated word meanings is _____.

29. Incorrect answers on multiple-choice tests are called _____.

30. Using ROY G BIV to remember the colors of the rainbow is a memorization technique known as a _____.

31. The process by which tests are analyzed to assess priorities is called _____.

32. Intensive review of selected items immediately prior to a test is called _____.

PART V: EXTENDED-ANSWER QUESTIONS (20 POINTS)

Answer two of the following.

33. Summarize the pros and cons of working with a study group.

34. List three primary learning modalities and give an example of how to work with each.

35. Enumerate the ways to cope with a panic attack during a test.

PART VI: ESSAYS (30 POINTS)

Answer two of the following.

36. Discuss in detail the criteria for writing good answers to essay questions.

37. Describe the causes of, effects of, and treatments for test anxiety.

38. Discuss in detail how to get more out of your reading.

Check your answers in the *Classroom Test Answers and Explanations* that follow. Grade your test. If your score is disappointing, look back in the book to locate the information you didn't know on the sample test. Then you'll know even more.

▶ CLASSROOM TEST ANSWERS AND EXPLANATIONS

PART I: IDENTIFICATIONS

1. a test on which a person's performance is judged in comparison to the performance of many others who took the same test

2. the part of the question that carries the information on which the question is based

3. memory tricks

4. learning in short segments over time

5. maps, charts, diagrams, or illustrations that show large amounts of information visually

PART II: TRUE/FALSE

6. F. *Connotation* is the associated meaning of a word.

7. F. The GED is a standardized test.

8. F. Distributed practice is intermittent and can't be used for cramming.

9. T. Monthly calendars show more time at a glance.

10. F. A study group should have no more than six members.

11. T. You may fall asleep if you study in bed.

12. T. Half of your time should be spent planning, and half should be spent writing.

13. F. *Visualization* is a relaxation technique.

14. F. Procrastination will only increase anxiety as the test taker delays his or her work.

15. T. Active voice is more powerful than passive voice.

16. F. A thesis statement is a preview of the main ideas of an essay.

17. F. Beware the absolute. *Never* is too strong a word.

PART III: MULTIPLE CHOICE

18. b. It is easier to memorize lists when you break them into groups of seven or any other uneven number.

19. d. All of the other choices are negative. This is the only one that suggests a reason that favors this question type.

20. c. If you don't listen to the instructions, you may miss valuable information from the instructor.

21. d. The big advantage of note cards is that they are portable.

22. d. Almost nothing is an absolute, so be careful of a statement that contains one.

23. a. The major virtue of graphic aids is the fact that they pack a lot of information in a small space.

24. d. Everything else will be easier if you are well organized.

25. b. The Internet contains a wealth of information about many standardized tests, including test dates.

26. c. Any kind of interference gets in the way of remembering what you are studying.

27. c. The layout of a monthly calendar allows for a broader view of a period of time.

PART IV: COMPLETIONS

28. Associated word meanings are *connotations*.

29. Incorrect answers on multiple-choice tests are called *distractors*.

30. Using ROY G BIV to remember the colors of the rainbow is a memorization technique known as a *mnemonic*.

31. The process by which test questions are analyzed to assess priorities is called *triage*.

32. Intensive review of selected items immediately before a test is called *cramming*.

PART V: EXTENDED-ANSWER QUESTIONS

33. Good reasons for a study group:

    a. Benefit of other peoples' ideas

    b. Sharing the workload

    c. Listening and talking to other students helps you remember

Drawbacks to study groups:

    a. Some members don't do the work.

    b. Some people socialize more than work.

    c. Some competitive people may not share their work.

34. Auditory learners learn by listening. They should say out loud what they are learning.

    Visual learners learn by seeing. They should color-code important information or map long ideas because they are easier to remember that way.

    Kinesthetic learners learn by doing. They should take lots of notes, underline, and make margin notes while reading.

35. Coping with a panic attack during a test:

    a. Put down your pen.

    b. Close your eyes.

    c. Relax completely.

    d. Breathe deeply.

    e. Visualize the end of the test.

    f. Make yourself more comfortable.

PART VI: ESSAYS

36. There are four main guidelines for writing essay answers on tests. Essay answers should be clear, concise, well organized, and accurate.

    In order to be clear on an essay, you should be familiar with the vocabulary of the topic on which you are writing. You should be aware of words that are easily confused, such as *advise* and *advice*, *affect* and *effect*, for example. You should choose words carefully and be sure that they mean what you want them to mean.

    You can be concise in your writing by keeping your sentence structure simple. You should use active voice whenever possible, and use verbs that are very specific to the sentence. Keep the language simple, and don't try to use extra words and phrases that repeat or pad the sentences.

    You can organize your essay answers by mapping or outlining the information quickly in the margins or on the back of the essay book. Be sure you start your essay with a good thesis statement, and start each paragraph with a topic sentence.

Your essay answers can be accurate if you pay attention to basic grammar and spelling rules. Make sure your sentences have the proper punctuation. Avoid the mistakes that take away from the content of your essay. These would include using *suppose to* instead of *supposed to* and using an apostrophe to make a plural. For example, "We had nice peach's today" is incorrect.

You can make a mnemonic like COCA (clear, organized, concise, accurate) to help you to remember the steps to writing a good essay.

37. Test anxiety comes from several sources and is different for each student. The effects of test anxiety can be simple or severe. Fortunately, there are ways of managing and sometimes curing test anxiety for most people.

The reason why some people suffer from test anxiety is that there are both real and imagined risks that they face when taking a big test. Real risks include failing to get into a school or job program or failing a course. In addition, we often imagine risks such as disappointing ourselves and others, facing an uncertain future, or repeating a previous failure.

For many people, test anxiety is mild and goes away once the test begins. For others, the effect of test anxiety is nervousness, sleeplessness, and fear of freezing up when they see the test. For some test takers, a little anxiety is good because it energizes them and makes them focus on performing successfully.

The treatments for test anxiety include confronting your fears openly, so you can deal with them. Sometimes, this means writing down the problem and then a solution, so you can see it in front of you and feel in control. A second treatment for test anxiety is overlearning, which means to study in such a way that the answers to questions are almost automatic. You should not make excuses for your performance on a test. Excuses make you a victim and take away your power over the test. You should also avoid procrastination in studying for your test. Don't hide behind defense mechanisms like rationalizing reasons for failure. And finally, you should visualize success on the test, and let that vision soften the effects of test anxiety.

38. Although most people believe that reading and retaining information is not a studied process, this is not the case. There are three steps you should take to make sure you comprehend and process what you read.

The first step to becoming a better reader is to pre-read. Pre-reading doesn't include only reading; it also involves thinking about what you will read and making decisions about it. So, first read the title. Based on the title, start thinking about what you will be reading. Is this a nonfiction piece? Is it going to try and persuade you to take some kind of action?

The second step to becoming a better reader is to become an active reader. You can accomplish this by taking notes as you read. Note taking forces you to think about and process the information. People who are auditory learners may prefer to take notes by speaking into an audiotape. This works, too, but may not be as convenient as writing down notes.

The third and final step to becoming a better reader involves post-reading. This simply means to think about what you read. Ask yourself, "What was interesting or useful about what I just read?" and "What did I learn from this reading?"

If you follow these simple three steps, you'll become a better reader in no time. Being a more efficient reader will help you when you take tests and complete reading assignments. It may even make you a better listener, too.

HOW WELL DID I DO ON THE PRACTICE CLASSROOM TEST? A SELF-ANALYSIS

I answered ___/5 questions correctly on the Identifications section.

I answered ___/12 questions correctly on the True/False section.

I answered ___/10 questions correctly on the Multiple-Choice section.

If I were the instructor, I would give ___/20 points for the Extended Answer responses.

If I were the instructor, I would give ___/30 points for the Essay answers.

I performed best on the _____ section(s) of
      the test.

I believe I did well on these sections because

I did not perform as well on the _____ section(s) of
      the test.

I believe I did not do as well on these sections because

To improve my performance on these sections, I need to

      _____ study more specific information (facts, terms, vocabulary).

      _____ study more general information (concepts, main ideas).

      _____ organize my answers more efficiently.

      _____ review spelling, usage, and punctuation rules.

Other   _____

             _____

You've learned a lot about how to take a test. Now it's time to assess how much you have learned about yourself and analyze the ways you'll work toward improving your test-taking skills even more.

Summing Up

R ight before the introduction, you took a test survey called "How Can I Get Smarter Than the Tests I Take?" Here are some quick answers for your review.

Multiple choice

Why are so many tests made in this format?
They are easier to grade and don't penalize poor writing or language skills.

How do I choose between two answers when they both seem right?
Try turning both answers into true/false questions.

Which should I read first, the questions or the answers?
If the question or stem is long, read the answers or options first.

How do I handle choices like "All of the above" or "None of the above"?
Read the stems carefully to note important terms, and always be wary of questions that are written as absolutes.

True/False

The statements always seem true to me. How do I know when a "true" answer is really false?
Note key words in the question very carefully. Make sure the statement is true in all circumstances.

Sometimes, part of the question seems true and another part seems false. How do I know which one to choose?
A true answer must be true in all of its parts.

Matching columns

Why do instructors sometimes put more answers than questions in a matching column section?
So you can't use process of elimination to determine an answer.

When two answers are very similar, how do I know which one to choose?
Answer all obvious choices first. Narrow your number of options.

IDs, fill-ins, or completions

How much information is required? I never know how much to say.
Put only the information that is required by the question. Don't take up valuable time padding an answer just to show off what you know.

What do I do if I know the answer but have forgotten the spelling?
Spell the word phonetically and hope that the instructor knows the word you mean.

What do I do if I remember only part of an answer?
Put down what you remember. You may get partial credit.

Essay questions

Why are essay questions so popular?
Essays allow students to display a range of skills and knowledge.

How do I make sure I don't run out of time when I write an essay answer?
Make a plan before you begin to write. Map or diagram your answer before you begin writing.

How do I figure out what to study before an essay test?

Rely on complete class notes, a thorough reading of all assignments, and special attention to points the instructor emphasized throughout the course.

In general

When—and how—should I guess on a test?

Guess when there is no penalty and when you have eliminated all but two possible answers.

How much time should I spend preparing for an exam?

This depends on how important the test is for your personal purposes, how much you already know, and your level of test anxiety.

If I have to cram for a test, how do I do it?

Limit the number of topics you study, make portable notes you can carry with you, and use multisensory means—seeing, hearing, and writing, for example—to learn the information faster.

Should I study with other people?

If you can study with well-disciplined friends or classmates in an organized and serious way, a study group can be helpful.

In the introduction, you were given a list of statements and asked to check off those that describe your test-taking abilities. Go back to that original list and take a look at those statements again, particularly those you checked off. What have you learned about yourself and about your test-taking skills since you began this book?

Let's find out. That list is repeated here. Read it again and find those statements that you checked off as true. Then, respond to the comments accompanying those statements. Look how far you have come!

1. *I am always nervous about tests.*

   Why do people get nervous on tests?

   In this book, what term is used for nervousness that's related to test taking?

   What can you do to cope with nervousness on tests?

2. *I am nervous on tests only when I don't feel confident about my performance.*

What can you do to gain the confidence you need to do well on a test?

3. *Sometimes the more I study, the worse I do on exams.*

Why does this happen?

How can you get more from your study hours?

4. *If I have time to study, I score better.*

What are some things you can do to manage time more efficiently?

5. *I do best on tests when I cram for them.*

What are the limits of cramming?

What are some strategies for cramming successfully if you must cram?

6. *When I take a test, I want to know the results immediately.*

Why is it important to you to get the results immediately?

7. *When I take a test, I don't want to know the results immediately.*

Why do you think you want to avoid seeing the test results?

8. *When I get nervous on tests, I freeze up.*

If you panic while you're taking a test, what are some things you can do to overcome your fear?

9. *I do better on essay questions than on short-answer questions.*

Why do you feel more comfortable with essay tests?

10. *I do better on short-answer questions than on essay questions.*

Why are short-answer tests easier for you?

11. *I do better on tests when I study alone.*

Why do you feel better when you study alone?

12. *I do better on tests when I study with a friend.*

How does working with someone else help you to study?

13. *I study better when I am in a quiet room.*

Why is it usually better to study in a quiet room than in a room with the radio or television playing?

14. *I study better when I play the radio or the television.*

What kind of studying can you do effectively when there is background noise in the room?

15. *Sometimes I am surprised when I get a lower score than I expected.*

How can you learn to be more informed about the tests you take?

16. *Sometimes I am graded unfairly.*

What is the best way to approach teachers about tests or about marks on a test?

17. *I sometimes get a better score on a test than I expected.*

Why are you sometimes surprised when you do well on a test?

18. *I sometimes do better on standardized tests than on classroom tests.*

Why are you more confident on a standardized test than on one that was written by your instructor?

19. *I sometimes do better on classroom tests than on standardized tests.*

How do you prepare differently for classroom tests than other tests?

How are standardized and classroom tests different from each other?

20. *Sometimes I study the wrong things for a test.*

How can you be as sure as possible that you are studying the right things for a test?

List three things you've learned about yourself as a student and a test taker as a result of reading this book.

_____

_____

_____

► KEEPING TABS ON YOUR PROGRESS

This book assumes that you will complete at least three to five practice tests in each area you want to review. These may include math, vocabulary, reading comprehension, analogies, problem solving, or spelling. Use the following chart to track your progress through your practice tests. Enter the number of questions you answered correctly in each test or section of a test. Enter the percentage of correct answers. When you have completed all the tests in each category that you intend to do, average your grades on all of the tests. (For examples, see the sample table that follows the blank one.) Finally, rate your performance in each category as:

S (satisfactory, no further review needed)
N (need some additional review)
U (need much more review)

Subject	Test 1	Test 2	Test 3	Test 4	Test 5	Average	Rating
	/	/	/	/	/		
	%	%	%	%	%		
	/	/	/	/	/		
	%	%	%	%	%		
	/	/	/	/	/		
	%	%	%	%	%		
	/	/	/	/	/		
	%	%	%	%	%		
	/	/	/	/	/		
	%	%	%	%	%		
	/	/	/	/	/		
	%	%	%	%	%		
	/	/	/	/	/		
	%	%	%	%	%		

SUGGESTIONS FOR TAKING PRACTICE TESTS

Follow the time limits set by the test. This will give you a realistic idea of how long it may take you to complete the test.

Use the results of the practice tests to determine the specific areas you need to spend more time reviewing.

Subject	Test 1	Test 2	Test 3	Test 4	Test 5	Average	Rating
English	43/75	58/75	63/75	60/75	68/75	77	N
	57%	77%	84%	80%	90%		
Math	50/60	52/60	54/60	56/60	58/60	90	S
	83%	86%	90%	93%	96%		
Reading	25/40	28/40	32/40	34/40	36/40	77	N
	62%	70%	80%	85%	90%		
Science	18/40	23/40	28/40	30/40	32/40	65	U
	45%	57%	70%	75%	80%		

This table was based on the four sections of the ACT 2000 test.

IN SHORT

If you've been following the 20-minute-a-day format, you've been working through this book for several weeks. You know it well—and you know yourself even better now. The strategies you've learned should help you to prepare for and take any kind of test, from a short-answer quiz in a classroom to a three-hour standardized college entrance test.

You're motivated to do well because you're eager to move ahead—in your life and with your education. The word *motivate* comes from a root word meaning *to move*. Let this book help you to move ahead.

So go for it, and take that test. Success is out there—within your reach!

Appendix A

THE ANSWER GRID

Most tests, either paper or electronic, use an answer grid on which answers are entered in "bubbles," small circle or ovals on the test page or screen. Here are some reminders on how to use an answer grid:

As always, read the directions carefully.

Make sure all bubbles are completely filled in.

If you want to change an answer, erase the first choice completely.

Make sure you don't leave extra marks on the paper.

And here is a suggestion: Some students find it difficult to keep track of which row of bubbles matches the question they are working on. A good way to work with this kind of grid is to mark all of the answers in a short section *in the book* or *on scratch paper,* and then transfer them all at once to the answer grid. You are less likely to lose your place on the answer sheet if you are entering a *group* of answers than if you are moving back and forth from test to answer sheet with each question.

1. ⓐ ⓑ ⓒ ⓓ ⓔ
2. ⓐ ⓑ ⓒ ⓓ ⓔ
3. ⓐ ⓑ ⓒ ⓓ ⓔ
4. ⓐ ⓑ ⓒ ⓓ ⓔ
5. ⓐ ⓑ ⓒ ⓓ ⓔ

Appendix B

ADDITIONAL RESOURCES

If you want more help with test taking, here are some resources you can use.

▶ BOOKS

You may find the following books helpful in preparing for a specific test or improving your study skills further.

STUDY SKILLS AND STRATEGIES

Basic Skills for College. New York: LearningExpress, 2001.

Critical Thinking Skills Success. New York: LearningExpress, 2004.

Paul, Kevin. *Study Smarter, Not Harder.* Bellingham, Wash., and North Vancouver, B.C.: Self-Counsel Press, 2002.

Robinson, Adam. *What Smart Students Know: Maximum Grades. Optimum Learning. Minimum Time.* New York: Three Rivers Press, 1993.

SPECIFIC SKILL AREAS

Essay Writing for High School Students: A Step-by-Step Guide. New York: Kaplan, 2006.

Express Review Guides: Basic Math and Pre-Algebra. New York: LearningExpress, 2007.

Express Review Guides: Grammar. New York: LearningExpress, 2007.

Express Review Guides: Vocabulary. New York: LearningExpress, 2007.

Express Review Guides: Writing. New York: LearningExpress, 2007.

Grammar Essentials, 3rd Edition. New York: LearningExpress, 2006.

Lerner, Marcia. *Math Smart, 2nd Edition.* New York: The Princeton Review, 2001.

Math Essentials, 3rd Edition. New York: LearningExpress, 2006.

Stewart, Mark Allen. *Words for Smart Test Takers, 2nd Edition.* Lawrenceville, N.J.: Arco, 2001.

Vocabulary and Spelling Success in 20 Minutes a Day, 4th Edition. New York: LearningExpress, 2006.

Write Better Essays in Just 20 Minutes a Day, 2nd Edition. New York: LearningExpress, 2006.

BOOKS ABOUT STANDARDIZED TESTS

Acing the GED. New York: LearningExpress, 2006.

Acing the SAT 2006. New York: LearningExpress, 2006.

ACT Preparation in a Flash. New York: LearningExpress, 2006.

Carnevele, Linda, and Roselyn Teukolsky. *Barron's SAT 2400: Aiming for the Perfect Score.* Hauppauge, N.Y.: Barron's, 2006.

McGraw-Hill's GED: The Most Complete and Reliable Study Program for the GED Tests. New York: McGraw-Hill, 2001.

SAT Math Essentials. New York: LearningExpress, 2006.

SAT Writing Essentials. New York: LearningExpress, 2006.

TOEFL iBT: The English Scores You Need! New York: LearningExpress, 2006.

▶ INTERNET RESOURCES

On the Internet, search engines such as Yahoo!, Ask, and Google can help you find publishers, tutors, and other sources of information that can help you prepare for and take a variety of tests. On www.freebooknotes.com, you can find links to websites that offer free book notes and summaries, literature study guides, and literary criticisms. For math practice, you can go to www.math.com to study topics, do practice exercises, and get helpful study tips.

LearningExpress offers a range of online products to help you prepare for exams and improve your skills in specific subject areas. Online courses include step-by-step preparation for the ACT, GED, and SAT, as well as interactive writing courses. You can also take practice tests that cover the different subject areas of the ACT, GED, and SAT, as well as general math, reading, and writing skills. You can purchase online products at www.learnatest.com. You may also be able to access them at your local library.

TUTORING

Some test takers feel that they need some one-on-one tutoring to prepare them for an important test. This may be true especially if there is a particular skill, like math or writing, that you feel that you may be weak in or that you need to improve with the help of a professional. Tutors advertise online, in local newspapers, on bulletin boards at schools and libraries, and in the yellow pages of the telephone book. If possible, it is a good idea to get a referral from someone who knows the tutor and his or her reputation in the community. Before hiring a tutor, be sure that you find out about his or her experience and expertise. Find out how long that person has been in the tutoring business. You may find someone who knows the subject well, but does not know how communicate knowledge in a patient and helpful manner. Private tutors are often quite expensive, so you owe it to yourself to find out as much as you can about a prospective tutor.

COMMERCIAL EXAM PREP COURSES

Thousands of students, old and young, enroll in the large exam prep courses offered for the SAT and other tests every year. These companies, such as The Princeton Review and Kaplan, offer tightly organized, programmed materials to assist in the preparation for college and professional examinations. Their courses are taught by enthusiastic, well-educated people who inspire students to do well and be successful on the tests. Often, the classes are supplemented by computer software and interactive learning labs available to customers. Courses such as these have a good reputation.

There are some drawbacks, however. These courses tend to be quite expensive and, therefore, are not an option for many test takers. Like anything else, getting the most—and the most for your money—requires a commitment by the learner to conscientiously use the CDs, study the words, and take the practice quizzes. For some people, the monetary investment is their motivation! For others, scheduling conflicts and other problems make it difficult to take full advantage of the program; they may have wasted money that could have gone to hiring a tutor or taking another kind of course.

NOTES

NOTES

NOTES

NOTES

NOTES